tragic blessing

Bret Merkle

Dedication

This work is dedicated to my Lord Jesus Christ
who turned my tragedy into blessing.
To my incredible Mom, who was my constant
comfort through the storm, and to my wonderful
wife, Marie, who has faithfully walked
with me every step of the way.

Acknowledgments

I could not have written this book without the unfailing support and counsel of my wife, Marie. Her constant encouragement kept me going, and she helped shape thoughts into words. I thank God for friends like Kristi Dawes who is an amazing editor; my friend, Alan Kent, for insights gained as we together learned how to walk again; and my parents and sisters for putting everything aside to help me get up after such a tragic fall in my life.

Foreword

I met Bret in college the year before his accident. When we met, Bret was extremely confident, possessed great strength, and had an impressive power that radiated from him. One day Bret was stripped of everything that defined him. I didn't know it then, but God had a perfect plan for Bret's life even though it would cause him much pain. Bret joins the great assembly of sufferers who endure pain for the sake of God's glory. His acceptance of God's plan has brought about unimaginable purpose for his life. With each step Bret now takes, he leaves behind a legacy. Whoever crosses his path is blessed by his walk with God and is inspired by the way he lives his life amidst his daily struggles.

- Marie Merkle

Table of Contents

Chapter 1 - Tragic

There was no time to react. My body slammed forward. The sound of metal scraping pavement pierced the air. The motorcycle tires crashed hard into a concrete curb, twisting and throwing me violently into a tree. Life was over as I knew it.

It was late in the evening, May 15, 1986. "Mr. and Mrs. Merkle? Oh yes, it's good to finally meet you," the surgeon said with a sigh. "The surgery went well. Bret made it through, but his spinal cord was badly damaged. Bret cannot move his legs, and he cannot feel anything below his waist. I'm so sorry to tell you this." There was a long pause. The air was tense with anticipation of what the doctor was about to say. He continued, "Your son. . . if he lives through this, he will never walk again. He will have to live the rest of his life in a wheelchair."

"Lives through this?" my father replied in disbelief. A large strong man with an imposing presence, he slumped back against the wall. I have two older sisters, but Dad wanted to continue having children until he got his boy. Now his boy lay there helpless, lifeless. A tough inner-city cop, he was normally in control of everything and everyone around him. But here, there was nothing he could do. He was out of his element.

My sister April stood listening with my parents. Slender and blonde, her thoughts raged in her head, "No! This can't be! Bret will die if he has to live in a wheelchair. Sports, football is all he knows! It's all he cares about!"

April's mind went back to October 1980. The night was dark with the cool, crisp October air dancing from her brother's mouth as he barked out the signals. "Set! . . . Red! Red! . . . 318! 318! Hut! . . . Hut, Hut!" The quarterback dropped back and rolled out to the right looking for his favorite target. Danny, a senior tight-end, shot out to the right flats and threw his hands high into the dark night air as the young quarterback pump-faked a pass to him. Pulling down his hands as if he caught the ball, Danny quickly made a sharp turn and sprinted downfield on a pump-and-go fly pattern. He was forty yards down field when suddenly the football was ten yards out in front of him. As the ball came down, Danny ran right under it catching the ball in full stride. The crowd roared as the sophomore quarterback just hit on his third touchdown pass of the game to beat the number one ranked team in the state. He was beginning to see his boyhood dreams come true. He was named All Conference that sophomore year and later named first team quarterback on the All State team for his junior and senior years.

Mom's voice broke through April's memories. "We'll make it through this, Bret," Mom said as she gently stroked my hair. Joanie, as everyone affectionately calls her, is from southern Missouri. Mom is quiet, loving and reserved. She and Dad both come from broken homes. Mom was raised by her grandparents after she was left behind by her unwed mother for a new family. Mom comes from the Bible-belt of America. She would need that strength to guide her family through this tragedy. Normally quiet and soft-spoken, Mom took charge to make sure her only son would get the best care possible.

* * *

My last memory was 3:00 a.m. the morning of the accident. It was the year the space shuttle exploded just after lift off and the first civilians ever to launch into space died before they even got there. My good friend, Bruce Crevier, and I had just climbed outside the window of our dorm rooms. We were both in our junior year at the University of South Dakota. The college campus of 6,000 students is in the small town of Vermillion, South Dakota, located in the southeastern corner of the state. We were goofing around trying to do back hand-springs and backflips, but mostly we were falling on our heads. It was a dark night in May 1986, and almost room temperature outside.

As we jumped, flipped and fell on our heads, a voice came out of the deep dark night. "Merrrrrk! . . . Merrrrk!" It was Doug's voice, All-American linebacker for the USD Coyotes. He lived a few doors down from me in the dorms and was coming back from an obvious night of celebrating. He could hardly stand up or walk straight. I was glad to see "Esch," as we all called him.

That was the last of my memory for another month to come. The next day I was in my dorm room full of anxiety over my last final exam. The class was Cobol computers. I hated the class and did not want to take the test. I had been blowing off studying for it and now I only had a day left to study before the test. Mindy stopped by and asked for a ride across town to get a paper from her grandfather's house. Mindy was a sweet girl, five foot, five inches tall with auburn-red hair and an athletic look. She especially liked riding on my motorcycle.

We left the dorms around four o'clock in the afternoon. It was a beautiful spring day. The smell of fresh-cut grass and spring flowers filled the air. I felt the anxiety of that final exam slip away as we took off racing through the dorm parking lot. There were few things in life I loved more than riding my motorcycle.

I grew up watching other neighbor kids riding motorcycles, but I had to ride my bicycle and pretend it had a motor on it. I even used clothespins to clip playing cards onto the front forks. The cards would hit the spokes of the tires and make a sound like a motor. I longed to ride my own motorcycle until age fifteen when I got my first one. It was a Honda motocross dirt bike. I spent most of the time riding it with the front wheel off the ground or jumping over ditch approaches.

Many times my friends would tell me, "Merk, you're going to kill yourself on that motorcycle someday!"

I usually responded by saying, "Yeah, that's fine. Just as long as I don't get all crippled up!" I did not realize what I was saying.

When I went off to college, I traded my dirt bike in for a street bike. I figured I needed to be more mature because I was going to college and a street motorcycle seemed to be what I needed.

That day turned out to be the last day of a normal life for me. We sped off on my motorcycle, a Suzuki GSL 850 cc. It was jet black and could flat out fly. I used to speed shift, spinning the back tire as the front tire left the ground. There was nothing in life more exciting. But I was driving more carefully than normal that day because I had a passenger. As we raced by the business school library, Bruce heard the sound of a motorcycle speeding past and looked up from his books to see us go by. Bruce had a motorcycle the same year, make and model as mine. We used to spend hours driving all over town and the countryside, but this time he was studying.

Mindy and I left her grandfather's house and headed back to the dorms. A car full of drunk college students was tailgating me. I sped up to put some distance between us, but they quickly sped up and were on my tail again in seconds. We could hear them yelling and screaming, honking the horn and revving their engine. Their car was swerving back and forth behind us as if they were trying to pass. Then they would get back on our tail.

We were quickly approaching another car in front of us. It was sitting in traffic with its left turn signal on, waiting for oncoming cars to clear so it could turn to the left across the traffic. I took the opportunity to get away from the drunken car party behind us, and I cracked the throttle wide-open speeding up to over fifty miles per hour as I swerved to the right to pass the waiting car. As quickly as I swerved, we were at the side of the car when it suddenly made a sharp turn right in front of us.

"No!" I yelled.

Smash! The motorcycle hit hard caving in the car's passenger side front fender.

Mindy flew over the top of me and onto the hood of the car, bouncing off and onto the street.

My body slammed forward into the motorcycle's gas tank. I hung onto the handlebars, instinctively trying to correct the force of the blow and ride out the collision to safety. The bike flew off the car, skidding and sliding on its side. People from several blocks away heard the ear-piercing sounds of metal scraping across the pavement as the bike carried me with it.

The tires suddenly hit the street curb, violently jolting and catapulting me forward. My head ripped past the handlebars, catching the mirror and ripping the flesh around my eye. I flew past the handlebars, twisting and flying forward, smashing into the solid three-foot trunk of an ash tree. My back hit first, wrapping me around the tree. I slid down the tree and crumpled lifelessly to the ground. I lay by the side of the tree with blood pouring out.

Mindy quickly got up and ran over to me. "Stay down, Bret," she said. "You're hurt, don't move! Just stay down," she demanded. Mindy was a capable and independent person. She took charge, trying to keep me from injuring myself worse.

Not listening, I tried to get up. I fought against her as she pushed on my chest to keep me down. Mindy's stomach grew sick as she saw me try to get up. Arms, hands, head and shoulders were all moving and struggling to get up, but my legs lay still without as much as a twitch or a flinch of movement.

Mindy knew immediately that something horrible was wrong.

"Oh God, Bret! Please just stay down. Please don't move," she begged.

Her heart sank realizing what just happened.

People came out of nearby houses and from all around after hearing the ear-piercing noise, curious to see the commotion.

"Call 911!" Mindy yelled. "Call 911! Hurry!"

"They're on their way," someone yelled back.

"What happened?" another asked.

"That's not Bret, is it?" another cried out.

Several minutes passed by after Bruce saw us race by the library. The familiar sound of piercing sirens broke the quiet of the library study. Bruce looked up and saw an ambulance race by. It was headed in the same direction Mindy and I had gone. Bruce made no connection in his mind to the ambulance and me on the motorcycle.

Twenty minutes later, Bruce was walking out of the library and a mutual friend came running up to him and frantically cried out, "Bruce! Bruce! Did you hear about Bret? He's been in an accident on his motorcycle."

"Where!" Bruce cried.

Together they sprinted three blocks and came to the scene. There, lying against the base of a thick ash tree in a pool of blood, was my mangled motorcycle. People were mingling around talking about what they had just seen. Bruce's heart dropped as he stared at the pool of blood. They had already taken me to the hospital.

The scene at the emergency room was chaotic. Doctors and nurses were rushing around trying to keep hoards of college students, interested friends and curious onlookers at bay. The small college-town hospital was not used to seeing trauma cases such as this one. I lay on the gurney cart in shock, lifeless. The injuries were too many to count and the blood continued pouring out. They knew I could not move or feel my legs, but that was the least of their worries. I was losing blood fast, and they could not find the source.

The average human body holds ten to twelve units of blood. When I arrived at the hospital, I had lost all but two. They immediately began to pump blood in me, but it was pouring out as fast as they could pump it in. Dozens of friends volunteered to donate their blood, but there was not enough of my blood type available.

Realizing they did not have the facilities and equipment to keep me alive, they rushed me to a regional trauma center in Sioux Falls, South Dakota. The ambulance blared away from the hospital as a doctor made the call to my family.

In a heavy German accent Dr. Krouch said, "Hello, Mr. Merkle?"

My father answered the phone in the back room of the small town bar we called home.

The doctor continued, "Your son has been in a terrible motorcycle accident here in Vermillion. He cannot move or feel his legs. He has a very bad injury to his head. The injuries are too many to list right now. We're sending him to the hospital in Sioux Falls. I am very sorry, Mr. Merkle, but your son may not make it there alive. You need to get there as fast as you can."

Stunned, my father hung up the phone and sank into a chair. He felt numb, not sure what to do or which way to go. He was in the back dining room of the family-owned business, a bar and restaurant. My father bought the business back in 1978 to get his family out of the crime and drug ridden city where I was born, Rockford, Illinois. He had been a police officer there for fifteen years and had seen more than enough bad things happen to kids. He wanted a better life for his children. When I was in eighth grade, he moved us to his hometown of Woonsocket, South Dakota, population 750, located in the central-eastern part of the state.

In a daze, Dad walked to his office to find my grandparents' phone number. Everything seemed to be moving in slow motion, as if it were a dream. Mom had left a week earlier to go visit her mother and step-father down in Missouri near St. Louis.

He dialed the number and waited for an answer.

"Hello?" Grandma answered.

"Juanita, is Joanie there? I need to talk to her right away," Dad inquired softly, his usual confidence gone.

"Why, yes, Don, she's here. Is everything all right?" Grandma asked.

Dad replied in nearly a whisper, "I just need to talk to her right away."

"She's right here," Grandma said, handing the phone to Mom.

"Yes, this is Joan. Don?" Mom inquired.

"Joanie . . . ?" Dad said with a hopeless, dull tone.

Mom declared, "It's Bret! It's Bret, isn't it? It's that motorcycle!" she demanded.

Mom had been having premonitions about me getting hurt on my motorcycle for the past month. Just before she left for Missouri, she sent me $100.00 to go buy a new motorcycle helmet. A girl from a small town close by, cute little Kimmy Higgins, had just been hurt in a motorcycle accident. Her neck was broken, paralyzing her from the neck down. Mom heard that if she had been wearing one of the newer-style helmets, she probably would not have been hurt so badly. Mom almost did not go to Grandma's because of those premonitions. Now they were coming true.

"Joanie, Bret's hurt really bad. His legs, his head. It's really bad, Joanie." Dad was still moving in a dream world.

"What's bad, Don? What is it?" Mom demanded more information.

"A car turned in front of him. He hit a tree. He can't feel his legs. He can't move them! They think his brain was injured too." He paused as he took a deep breath and continued, "He's losing blood. They're rushing him to the hospital in Sioux Falls. We need to get there right away. The doctor said to get there before . . . "

Mom cut him off. "I'm leaving right now. I'll be there tonight."

Her bags were already packed. She was leaving Grandma's to go stay with her sister for a few days in St. Louis. Mom was on the plane headed back home within hours.

As she was sitting on the plane, her thoughts whirled around in her mind. "Will I ever see Bret again alive? How bad is it? He's strong. He's a fighter. He'll make it. I know He will!"

She prayed, "Lord, I can't let him go yet. He's my boy. Lord? Please, Lord, no! Don't take him yet. Please, let him live. Just let him live. . ."

Mom always had a quiet faith. She kept a diary from the first day of the accident. She wrote:

May 15, 1986: Accident!! Called at Mom's. Praying!! Praying!! Got to fight back. I feel like someone socked me in the stomach.

Chapter 2 - Paralyzed

The news hit the people of my small hometown like a ton of bricks. Just a few years earlier I headed off to college on a scholarship to play football and baseball. When you are from a small town, everyone knows all about you, especially when your family owns a business on main-street. I also coached little league baseball and taught swimming lessons. It was like a big family. The news of my accident spread like a forest fire. People in droves were coming to our family-owned bar, Don's Silver Dollar, to see what they could find out. Others were walking the streets in complete disbelief and bewilderment.

On the other side of the world, my sister Jana was living on an Air Force base in England. She was at a birthday party and had left an emergency phone number where she could be reached. Jana's friend, Jackie, took the call and immediately gave the phone to Dave, Jana's husband. Her stomach sank as she saw Dave take the call.

Her mind was racing, "Is it Grandma? Grandpa? What's wrong?" Her mind continued to swirl with fear, "Grandma must be in the hospital again. Or Grandpa had another stroke."

"Jana, honey, let's go in here," Dave tenderly escorted Jana into a side bedroom and shut the door.

"It's your Mom," Dave explained, sitting next to her on the bed and handing her the phone. The feeling in her stomach changed to nausea.

"What? Mom, what's going on?" she demanded softly, nearly in tears already. She knew it had to be bad. "Just tell me what's going on."

Mom answered, "Jana, It's Bret."

"Bret? What? Is he okay?" Jana pleaded.

"Your brother is in the hospital. We're in Sioux Falls. He . . . ahhh, well he's been in ahhh . . . a motorcycle accident." Mom, now at the hospital with the rest of the family, said with a reassuring tone in her voice. Mom and Dad decided not to tell Jana the complete story, not wanting to worry her for the long flight home.

"You and Bret, well . . . you were so close. It's the doctors. They . . . they think it could really help Bret if you could be here. Do you think you can come home?" Mom explained.

"Yes, yes!" Jana sobbed. She could hardly get out the words, "I . . . I'll, I'll ask for, for emergency leave. I'm sure I can get it. I'll try right away." She continued, "Mom, is he going to be all right?"

"Yes, Jana. They're doing all they can. They say he's doing very well," Mom said as she tried to hide the truth.

The staff sergeant's office was cold and bare. Jana's staff sergeant busily worked with his clerk to finish the paperwork for the emergency leave. The familiar sound of a fax machine rang out as the fax came through from the hospital. The staff sergeant pulled the paper from the fax and began to read.

With a quick, firm step, he walked over to his staff clerk's desk. Placing it in front of him, he ordered, "Corporal, we've got to move. This girl's brother is dying in a hospital in South Dakota. We have to get her there ASAP. Hopefully she'll make it before he's gone."

The staff sergeant did not realize Jana and Dave were sitting on the other side of the paper-thin partition wall separating the waiting room from the work area. She could hear his voice clearly. Those words pierced her heart. The flight home was longer than she could have imagined.

May 16: The hall is full of kids all full of panic.
I'm moving in a dream. No sleep. All family is here.
Called Jana and Dave. She sobbed so hard. All we
can do is pray!!

* * *

Marjorie was an elderly lady who worked around the dorms cleaning up after all of us. We loved to tease and have fun with her. We tried to include her and make her feel at home. Marjorie bumped into Bruce as he was walking out of his dorm room the morning after the accident. She said with a sad voice, "Bruce, I'm so sorry to hear about your friend Bret."

Bruce answered with a quiet sadness in his voice, "Yeah." Looking down, he shook his head and continued, "He was in a terrible motorcycle accident. He's in the hospital. I guess he's hurt pretty bad."

"Oh, my!" she said with surprise in her voice, "You haven't heard yet?"

"Heard what?" Bruce asked.

"I'm so sorry," she continued, "Your friend died last night."

"What? No!" Bruce cried out as he ran to the nearest phone.

Bruce immediately called the hospital and asked the nursing staff if the news was true.

"Why, no," a nurse replied with a caring tone, "Bret is still alive. But he is touch and go every hour."

Bruce was relieved but shocked about what he was hearing. That kind of news was running all over the college campus. Many were hearing similar stories. There had been a false radio report the night of the accident leaving many friends in shock and disbelief.

Mark was another friend who heard the news. He was with some others who had been turned away by the hospital staff when they tried to visit earlier that day. They were together at another friend's house talking about everything that had happened. As they were talking, a local radio station broke into a news report. The room suddenly became very quiet as they listened to the report. "Bret Merkle, a junior student at USD, was fatally injured earlier today when his motorcycle collided with a car. He died from severe head, back and internal injuries."

"No!" Mark yelled as he ran to a phone to dial the hospital. Mark's heart pounded as his fingers hit the numbers on the phone. Sobs and cries of disbelief rolled across the room like a wave. It all seemed to happen so fast. Just days earlier, we were all at a party together celebrating the end of another school year. The sting of death and its finality hit hard.

Mark talked with one of the ladies on the nursing staff who was feeling more like a telephone operator from all of the phone calls about the news report. She patiently told him that it must have been a false report. Mark was relieved but deeply hurt to hear how serious the injuries were. Mark's cousin had just been paralyzed from the neck down in a diving accident the previous year, and he knew all too well what lay ahead.

* * *

I was slipping closer and closer to death each day as the doctors performed surgery after surgery to save my life. The first emergency surgery was to put my eye back in its socket. The force of the impact left it lying on the side of my face. The tissue around the eye and my forehead was so badly shredded the surgeon was doubtful I would be able to see out of the eye. From there, they rushed me into another surgery to stop internal bleeding. Blood was pouring into my stomach from the pelvic area. It was broken in four places. They cut me open from my chest down below my belly button.

I was in good physical shape since playing sports was a big part of my life. Working out with weights was a daily event up until the accident. I was overly concerned about my physique at that time, like most other twenty-one-year-old young men. But all that hard work lifting weights and working out was now my best ally in the fight to save my life.

My pelvis was crooked from the break. The only way to fix it was to place me in traction. That was out of the question because there were so many other problems needing immediate attention. The vertebrae in my lower back were broken. An orthopedic surgeon, Dr. Benson, moved the vertebra back into place relieving the pressure off the damaged spinal cord. He bolted long steel rods, called Harrington rods, on each side of the spine to hold it together.

The spinal cord was badly bruised but not severed, which was good news. Medical science had not figured out how to repair a severed spinal cord with all of its many tiny nerves making up the cord. Dr. Benson told my family the spinal cord was like a wire that runs from a light switch to a light. He explained that when the wire gets cut, there is no way the signal can get from the switch to the light. The same goes for the spinal cord. When the cord gets cut or bruised, messages from the brain cannot travel to the muscles telling them to move.

Dr. Benson explained further, "We know from medical science and from all the statistical studies that when the spinal cord is damaged like Bret's, there is only a one percent chance he'll ever walk again." He continued, "His back is stabilized for now, but he has a more serious problem. Bret's blood pressure is 50/20. We're not sure how he's doing it, but he's hanging on."

They took me back to the Intensive Care Unit for more tests. I was still losing blood. In all, there had been thirty-eight units of blood pumped through me, nearly four times what the body holds. The blood was literally just passing through and the blood loss could not be explained. It seemed there was a timebomb ticking, but they did not know where.

May 16: Back surgery. Praying. Damage to the spinal cord!! Lord, help us all! Bret is fighting so hard. He's so strong. I know he'll make it.

A bright young nurse taking care of me was off work when certain routine tests had been cancelled. Not knowing that, she drew blood to run the tests. Afterwards, she looked at the blood she had drawn. Seeing bubbles in the blood, she knew something was wrong. She went to the doctor right away.

Dr. Schultz, another surgeon in charge of my overall care, knew immediately what the bubbles meant. Air was somehow getting into the blood system. That could only mean one thing. It meant the force of the impact must have torn a blood artery or even the heart itself. He found the timebomb they were looking for! Dr. Schultz knew it should have exploded long before. There was no time; he had to get to it before it blew.

He rushed to my family and began to explain, "Bret must have something in or near his heart that was torn open. That is where the blood must be coming out. He is losing blood pressure fast."

With a strong sense of urgency Dr. Schultz continued to explain, "We have to get in there before his heart stops. We'll be taking him now. You may want to say your final goodbyes. I'm sorry. I just can't say if he'll make it through this surgery. He should not have lived this long with that problem."

May 17: Praying!! No time for anything!! Must get to it before it breaks. Blood pressure and vitals no good. Bret may die! Oh, God!!

The family gathered around as I lay waiting to be taken into another emergency surgery. Mom took my hand and said in a firm voice, "Bret, you've always been a fighter. Fight to get through this one."

She felt guilty because she was asking me to do it for her more than anything. She could not bear to lose her only son. They wheeled me into the surgical room and Mom hugged Grandma tightly. Grandma had just flown in from Missouri.

"Mom," she sobbed, "Is it okay? Is it right for a mother to hang on so tightly?"

Grandma replied softly, "Joanie, as long as there is hope. And as long as it is God's will, yes, it is right."

Dr. Schultz made the incision from the bottom of my left shoulder blade across the top of my back. The familiar sound of the heart monitor, "Beep . . . Beep . . . Beep" continued until the moment he could see my heart. Just then, the familiar sound went off, "Beeeeeeeeeeeeeeee." My heart stopped beating, the blood pressure finally had fallen to the fatal level.

"We have to move! Move! Get me the pressurizer! What's his blood pressure?" Dr. Schultz screamed out orders. The surgical room was moving at a dizzying pace as the other doctors, nurses and attendants moved with precision and skill to pressurize my heart.

"Where is it? I can't see! Clear that blood out of there! I can't see where it's coming from!" Dr. Schultz ordered. "More suction!" he screamed.

The suction tube cleared out the blood. He saw the timebomb! It was a tear in the aorta leading directly out of the heart. The tear let the blood leak out, allowing the pressure to drop so far that the heart could no longer pump. He found it just in time. The sound, "Beeeeeeeeeeeee" continued for nearly a minute as Dr. Schultz quickly and skillfully repaired the tear with a Teflon wrap, allowing the blood system to pressurize.

It began beating again, "Beep, beep, beep." Relieved by another close call, Dr. Schultz slowly finished the repair by carefully sewing the Teflon material around the aorta.

After the surgery, Dr. Schultz explained what had just happened. "It was a miracle. The timing of it all," he told them. "When a person has a torn aorta, they usually don't make it to the hospital alive. Bret made it three days with a hole in his aorta. I can't believe it! It's like trying to drive on a tire with a hole in it. All the pressure leaks out and the tire goes flat. It is the same with a torn aorta injury. The blood system loses pressure, and the heart stops beating. Bret is a very lucky boy." He continued, "Believe me, there are virtually no survivors if the torn aorta is not found within twenty-four hours. We did not find Bret's torn aorta for three days while he went through three other major surgeries! I don't know how his heart continued beating through it all. I cannot explain that from the medical standpoint."

May 17: Surgery 6 hours. Came through this one.
Blood pressure and vitals no good.

Jana, a year older than me, came into the ICU room as soon as she and Dave made it to the hospital from England. The family greeted them in the hallway just outside the intensive care unit.

"Jana, you need to prepare yourself before you go in there," Mom urged.

"Mom, I know it's bad. I'm ready. I've come all this way. I have to see him," Jana replied calmly.

Jana, clad in her Air Force dress blues, quietly walked to the bedside. I was lying upside down in a striker bed frame, which is a special bed for patients who are paralyzed. The nurses came in to flip me over every few hours in order to prevent bed sores as they contended with many tubes and machines keeping me alive. Jana got down on the floor and crawled under the bed, lying on her back so she could see me. She was my best friend growing up, a constant source of strength. Seeing her meant everything was going to be okay.

"Hey, little brother. How ya doin' up there?" she said softly as her deep brown eyes connected with mine. I have always drawn strength from her eyes. No matter what the situation, I always saw hope in her eyes.

"Jana, don't worry about me," I responded in nearly a whisper and with an unexpected tone of hope in my voice. "God let this happen so I could go tell the world about Jesus!" I reassured her.

Jana hid her surprise, thinking that kind of comment had to come from the drugs. She did not know how I had changed while I was at college due to my newly found relationship with Jesus. We come from the kind of home that never discussed religion. It wasn't that we did not believe, it was just that God and Jesus were not a part of our lives, especially for me. I would have rather argued with someone about the legitimacy of Bible stories than approach faith as a child. Jana took that into account when I mentioned Jesus. Neither one of us knew the significance of that statement.

May 18: Constant fight to live. He's fighting so hard.

The enormous blood loss was beginning to take its toll, causing the major internal organs to fail. One by one they were shutting down. First the kidneys, then the lungs. The nursing staff was working overtime to keep my organs from shutting down. Just when they would get one organ hooked up to a machine to keep it going, another organ would begin to fail.

It was an emotional rollercoaster for my family and friends. One minute they were told I was slipping away and would probably not make it much longer. The next minute they were told I was coming back and fighting hard to survive.

May 19: Crisis night. Bret came back to us. Kidneys and lungs failing. Praying so hard. God help us!!

The pressure on the family was building. Tiptoeing on the edge of life for several days is unbearable for family members with nothing to do but watch and wait. There was nowhere to go for rest other than the waiting room, which made it even harder. By now it had been five days and everyone had gotten little sleep.

May 20: Lungs failed. All of us are sleeping and staying in ICU waiting room.

My family slept in a small waiting room for weeks while I was slipping in and out of death's door. This tragedy was not only threatening my life, it was taking a heavy toll on my family as well. God was working in each one of us in our own individual ways.

*May 23: Bret is fighting the tube in his throat. He
pulled the tube out. He's back on oxygen.*

An oxygen tube was placed in my throat so I could breathe.
There were many small battles going on alongside the war. The
oxygen tube for me was one of those small side battles. I was forced
to write notes on a pad of paper to communicate.

I fought that oxygen tube, and I was fighting the nursing staff
that was trying to keep it in. Dad walked in on one such nurse after
the battle had been raging for over a week. She was on her knees
with her back to the door. I was lying on the striker bed facing the
floor. Dad walked in and thought it was odd that she had pulled
the curtain shut since I did not have a roommate.

He peeked through the curtain. He saw her squeeze my wrist
and pin it against the bed rail. With her other hand she quickly wrapped a white bandage around my arm, tying it down. She
pulled and jerked the bandage, tying it tightly. The other arm was
already tied down.

As she was tying my wrist to the side of the bed he heard her
say, "There! You won't pull that thing out again!"

Dad, being the fighter, jumped to my rescue. She startled when
he yelled, "What in the *#!%* are you doing? Get out of here before I throw you out!"

She was never seen on the ICU floor again.

*May 24: Praying! How much more can Bret
handle?*

Blood clots were developing in my lungs. They took me in for
more surgery to clear my lungs. The procedure lasted much longer
then expected. Since it was taking so long, Mom left the rest of the
family in the waiting room and walked down the hall. She was ner-
vously standing outside the surgical room, wondering why it was
taking so long. Dr. Schultz finally came out.

She was standing alone by the wall with her arms folded across her body. "Mrs. Merkle, is there any other family near by?" he asked.

"No, they're in the waiting room. What is it?" she questioned with an anxious tone. "You can tell me. Just be straight with me. We didn't lose him, did we?" she pled with him demanding to know.

Looking down at the floor to avoid eye contact he said, "His heart stopped again. He's so weak. He's been through so much." He explained further, "I just don't know how much longer he'll make it."

Mom was at the end of her rope. The constant tension and stress of the past two weeks going from one surgery to the next, hoping and waiting, had worn her out. Just when one bit of news came from the doctors offering a glimmer of hope, more news came that shattered what little hope was left. Day after day she was hanging on to every word from the doctors hoping the nightmare would end.

Dr. Shultz consoled her and quietly left. She thought to herself as she stood alone in the hallway, "This isn't fair to Bret. I have to let him go."

My father, whose optimism was a cover for his denial, walked over just as Dr. Schultz explained what had happened. "So, how's the battle?" he asked with a made up confident voice.

"Don," Mom replied in a tone that meant business, "Bret's heart stopped again." Her frustration about his denial was beginning to show.

He fell back against the wall, shocked at the news. He was shaken by the sudden revelation of reality. "What? I thought we were past that," he exclaimed.

"Don, I have been trying to tell you. It's not that easy. Bret is going to die unless there is some kind of miracle. No one can make it through all this," Mom said as she tried to convince him. She was frustrated as she tried to deal with his denial.

May 28: Bret in for lung scope. Heart stopped.
Returned to us again.

Later that night Dr. Schultz sat with the family trying to explain. "It has now been two weeks. The human body is not designed to take all that Bret is going through. He's had a severe loss of blood and the internal organs are shutting down." He paused and continued, "Bret has nothing left to fight with. He's lost most of his strength from so many surgeries in such a short period of time. I don't see how he will make it through the night. I am so sorry. We have done all we can."

> *May 28: Bret's temp too high. Going to the cooling*
> *bed. Praying for Bret. How much more can he*
> *stand? How much more will God put on this boy? I*
> *wonder if it is right to hold on so tight.*

Mom knew what she had to do. There was a small chapel near the ICU waiting room. She went into the chapel by herself. Sitting on the small pew, she looked up to a picture of Jesus on the cross. She felt like He was in the room with her.

She prayed, "Lord, this is so hard. I can't do this without Your help." She continued, "Lord, I am giving Bret to you. He is in Your hands now." She finally let go. It was over.

Mom stayed in the chapel a while longer feeling like she was in the presence of God. For the first time since she received the call at her mom's house in Missouri, she felt peace. It was almost as if the storm were over. She wondered if it was. She was certain her son was gone.

> *May 28: This is the day to turn Bret over to God.*
> *I have.*

Chapter 3 - Darkness

The long hallway was dark with soft baseboard lights lighting the floor as Mom walked towards the intensive care unit. The dark hallway matched Mom's feeling inside. She thought to herself, "This must be what it feels like when a mother loses a child." Yet the soft lights that lit her path were symbolic of the peace she felt from the night before when she turned her son over to God.

It was six o'clock a.m. Most of the patients were not up yet. Dr. Schultz was standing at the nurse station. "Have you seen Bret yet?" he asked.

"No I haven't," Mom replied.

"I don't know how to tell you this," Dr. Schultz continued.

That familiar sick feeling immediately returned. It was a sinking feeling in her stomach. She knew this was it. She knew her son was gone. She almost could not breathe.

"I don't know how to explain it. It's as different as day and night. He is so much better today," Dr. Schultz explained.

The sick feeling left as quickly as it came. It was replaced with a flood of relief. "What? What do you mean?" she begged for more information.

"Like I said, I can't explain it. He is doing so much better today," he replied.

Mom knew in her heart what had happened. Her thoughts went to the chapel the night before. The peace she felt after placing her son in God's hands was now confirmed. She had been fighting the decision to do it since she had gotten the call at Grandma's. She thought it meant she had to accept death, that if she entrusted her son's life into God's hands He would take him from her. But now she knew it did not mean that at all! Instead, it simply meant to trust and have faith.

"It's a miracle," Mom said as she hugged Dr. Schultz. He offered his usual quiet smile, not wanting to offer false hope.

* * *

The next wave in the storm was about to hit. Mom saw a reddish-colored streak going up my right leg. "I have been watching this for the past several days. It seems to be getting worse," Mom said to a nurse as she changed an IV bag.

"Yes, it does look like it is getting worse," the nurse said as she examined it. "It is running higher up his leg. I will tell the doctor."

A short time later, a special bed designed to cool off the body and control rising body temperature was wheeled into the room. They transferred me onto the cooling bed, turning it down to its coldest temperature. As I lay on the cooling bed, nurses added IV bags to pump more antibiotics into my veins. They were trying everything they could to bring down my body temperature, which was hovering around 106 degrees.

It was Memorial Day weekend. The hospital was more like a morgue than a health care facility. There were no doctors available to look at my leg with the growing concern of infection. Finally, when the weekend was over they ran some tests including a CAT scan to see what was going on.

Dr. Witzkie, another wonderful surgeon, gave me excellent care. He examined my leg and realized the infection was at a critical stage. He decided I needed more surgery. The orderlies wheeled me out of my room on a surgical cart and down the hall to the surgical floor.

Dr. Witzkie talked with my family as they took me away. "This procedure is called "debrisment" surgery," he explained. "The infection has advanced tremendously in the past few hours. If we don't get that infection out of there, it will get into his blood stream and kill him."

"What will the surgery do?" April asked.

"We have to cut out any tissue that the infection has already killed. Hopefully it's not much." Dr. Witzkie continued to explain the procedure to the family, but they were not prepared for what was about to happen.

May 29: Bret talking clear today. Put on body
brace. Temp up. Leg and foot infected.

The surgery lasted several hours. I woke up from surgery and saw several people standing by my bed talking. I was not sure who they were. One of them sounded like Dr. Witzkie. I was not sure if I was dreaming or not. They were looking over my leg and talking about it.

"There's not much left," Dr. Witzkie explained. "I don't see how we can save it."

I heard words, but I could not understand. It was like they were talking in a different language. It seemed like they were far away.

"How's it look?" I muttered, still groggy from the anesthesia.

"Oh, I thought you were still out," Dr. Witzkie said with his usual frankness. "The surgery is all done. It does not look good. You need to seriously consider amputation. You may not have a choice. I would recommend that . . ."

I drifted back to sleep while he was still talking to me.

Dr. Witzkie walked out of my room. Stepping into the hallway he saw Mom. "Hello, Mrs. Merkle. I was just talking to Bret. I'm sorry, but we really are not left with much choice. We need to amputate," he explained plainly without emotion.

"You didn't tell Bret that, did you?" Mom worriedly replied.

"Well, we were talking about it, but he fell asleep on me," he answered.

"It's just not that simple. It's not just something you can throw away. That's his leg you know," Mom said with frustration.

"Have you seen his leg?" Dr. Witzkie inquired.

"No. Should I?" Mom asked.

"Yes. Then you'll know what I'm talking about," he replied confidently.

Mom went to get Dad. He and Jana were in the ICU waiting room. "Bret is waking up and we need to see his leg," Mom told them. Together they walked to the room. Shelly, my night nurse, just finished removing the gauze and bandages. Mom, Dad and Jana slowly walked into the room. My leg was propped up on pillows as I lay in bed sleeping.

They saw my leg. It was cut wide open with gaping holes from the knee down to the ankle. They could see the bone as they looked past open flesh, muscle fibers and tissue. Some of it was pink in color. Other parts were a dark blackened color.

Skin had been removed along the top of the foot. The small bones on the top of the foot from the ankle to the toes were a brilliant white color lying against redish-pink flesh. It looked like one of those pictures seen in a doctor's office showing the human body's muscles and fibers without the skin covering it. The heel pad had been completely removed leaving a deep dark cavity in its place.

Mom and Dad looked at the leg, then looked at each other. Debrisment surgery was much more than they expected. They both thought it simply meant "cleaning" out the infection, not cutting half the leg away.

"Oh, Lord!" Mom said softly as she stared. "What happened?" she asked.

"We had no choice. The tissue we cut away was already dead. If we left it, the infection would have spread even faster," Dr. Witzkie explained.

Mom was angry. She was mad at the doctors, the nurses, the hospital, and the whole world. She noticed the red streak weeks earlier, but they said nothing could be done because everything else was more important. She retraced in her mind all the surgeries, the procedures and treatments over the past three weeks. At first it only looked like a deep bruise on the ankle. They told her it was an "impact burn," which was a crushing-type injury. She watched each day as the redness grew, but they would not do anything about it. "Now it's too late. It's gone. There's no turning back!" she cried in her mind.

Dad stood in utter disbelief wishing he could trade places, yet there was nothing he could do. Denial was forced from his mind by the sheer horror of what he saw. He wanted this to be over.

> *May 29: Leg worse. Removed all dead area! Oh,*
> *God! Talk of amputation. NO!! They want to make*
> *a decision on using legs.*

Dr. Witzkie continued to explain, "We are going to have to clean this diligently. We'll have to scrub the leg every four hours until it's clean. Once it's clean, we'll have to do a muscle graft surgery. It has never been done in this part of the country. Actually it has only been done a handful of times in the world. It is extremely risky."

He moved over next to me and continued, "We will need to cut this large muscle out of Bret's back." Pointing to my back, just under the right arm he said, "Right there." Continuing, he said, "We'd have to cut this muscle out and graft it into the open areas in his leg."

Moving down to my leg he continued, "If that works, we will take a large amount of skin off his upper legs." Pointing to the thigh area of my legs he explained, "We'll use that skin to cover the new muscle graft area. But Bret's main problem is his heart." He paused, "It's just too risky to put him through another major surgery, eight to ten hours, as weak as he is. His heart has already stopped during lesser procedures." He continued, "It will be much safer to let us amputate his leg once he is stable and has regained some strength."

* * *

After I woke up, Mom, Dad and Jana came in to talk to me. "Bret, we have to talk to you about something." They walked over and stood by my side. I was awake from the surgery watching the nurse work on my IV bag when they came in. I looked down at my leg and saw bandages from above the knee all the way to my toes. Dad had a look on his face that I had never seen before. He looked meek and humble, almost as if he were scared.

Standing next to me by the bed he said with a boyish uncertain tone, "Bret, we just talked to Dr. Witzkie. He . . . he says, auhh. Your leg. Well, it's really bad. He's not sure . . . He can't say . . . He's not sure if he can save it."

Suddenly I was wide awake. I heard every word. "What! Not save it? I can't lose my leg. They can't! You won't!" I cried, trying to sit up in the bed as I protested. I reached for something to grab as I strained to get up. I quickly lost strength in my struggle. My head felt dizzy. The room began to spin round and round. I felt sick. My head fell back against the pillow.

I saw Jana at the end of the bed. Suddenly I was back home in Woonsocket. I was normal again. The gymnasium was loud where the pep rally was held. Earlier that day I rode in the back of a 1965 Mustang convertible in the homecoming parade on main street. There were six of us chosen for homecoming royalty. Three boys and three girls. We were the Woonsocket Redmen. Two of us were to be crowned Homecoming King and Queen at the coronation later that night.

The music was loud and the atmosphere was electric. It seemed Woonsocket was the center of the universe back then. Nearly the whole town turned out for the Homecoming festivities. We were to play the number one ranked team in the state, and we were the underdog rated number four. I liked that.

The drums beat loudly and the trumpets sounded off playing our high school theme song. All the royalty candidates sat on the floor wearing Native American dress. The school principal read the names of the Homecoming King and Queen.

He announced loudly, "This year, Woonsocket's Homecoming King and Queen are . . ." he paused as the drum rolled, "Bret Merkle and Lori Olson!" The crowd roared in approval, kids yelling and screaming with parents clapping. The principal crowned Lori with a beautiful queen's leather beaded headband and me with a brilliant colored full feathered chief's headdress. I could not wait to get out there and beat the number one ranked team in the state!

"Bret, are you okay?" Mom's voice broke through my thoughts stopping my day-dream.

That sick feeling in my stomach quickly returned as I was pulled back into reality. This was my new world now, that old world seemed a lifetime ago. I longed to go back. Tears came down my face. I could not speak. All I could do was slowly turn my head from one side to the other hoping they would understand.

> *June 2: Blood count is down, white cells up. I am really worried tonight. Bret upset. Leaving it in God's care. This is the only way I can survive. Waiting and praying.*

* * *

In private, outside of where I could hear conversation, Dr. Witzkie discussed the amputation with my family. "We need to be realistic. If Bret were not paralyzed I would agree that it may be worth it to try and save his leg. The orthopedic and neurosurgeons tell us that he will never walk again anyway. If that is the case, why put him through it? It is too risky," he reasoned.

"Well, what is so risky about it?" Mom asked naively.

Dr. Witzkie tried his best to explain. Dad replied, "Doctor, I know what you are saying, but you don't know my son." He looked at the doctor with sincerity, "He would rather die than lose his leg. He will fight this and he will never give up." With that said, they agreed to move forward with trying to save my leg.

The scrubbings began that day.

* * *

A different nurse came into my room. There were so many I lost track. Dr. Witzkie followed.

"Hello, Bret. We're going to clean your leg and put on new dressings," she said with a smile.

I watched wondering what was going to happen. She slowly unwrapped the bandages. I had not yet seen my leg since the debrisment surgery. As she continued, I looked closely to see what she was doing. With all the bandages off, she began to pull out dark blood-soaked gauze that had been packed in my leg. I could not believe what I saw as the last pieces of gauze came out. My stomach grew sick.

I could see gaping holes in my leg! "What did you do to me? It's gone! Half my leg is gone!" I screamed in protest.

I closed my eyes not wanting to watch. I prayed, "God, let me die! Please God, let me die!" I could not imagine going through life like this! "This is not me . . . It can't be!" I cried in my mind.

I felt something near my leg and opened my eyes again. The nurse began scrubbing the exposed flesh and bone with a scrub brush. I grabbed the side rails on the bed to brace myself. She was scrubbing with a brown colored solution. I heard the brush scrubbing as she made short quick movements back and forth, back and forth. I felt the bristles of the brush. It was a dull sensation in some areas and sharper in others.

It was all happening so fast. "Is that my leg?" I thought in disbelief. "This can't be . . ."

She continued scrubbing. I felt sharp pains as the brush hit certain areas. Then it happened. She was scrubbing deep into an exposed cavity near the bone. There were live nerves in there, open and raw! The scrub brush hit a nerve that was fully alive! It felt like a lightening bolt shot through my leg.

I bit down hard and turned my head to the side trying not to cry or scream. The nurse continued to scrub and scrub. I anticipated each swipe of the scrub brush bringing another lightening bolt

30

of pain. Then it happened again. Then again. Sweat was pouring out of me like a fountain.

During those scrubbings I learned to crawl into a hiding place in my mind. I fought going there at first. That meant the pain was completely intolerable. At some point during the scrubbings I drifted into my hiding place where I found warmth and safety. It literally felt like I left my body and drifted away.

"He stilled the storm to a whisper;
the waves of the sea were hushed."
- Psalm 107:29

The scrubbing took twenty minutes. "It's over!" I whispered, exhausted.

Finally I breathed easy as I watched the nurse pack gauze back into the holes. She wrapped it again with gauze and bandages. When finished, she could not help but notice my hospital gown and bedding were soaked with sweat. As she changed my gown and bedding, I looked at the clock. It was twenty minutes after the hour. Suddenly I could not breathe again. I remembered they told me it had to be scrubbed every four hours for the next thirty days. That meant another one in only three hours and forty minutes.

I was in for the darkest, most painful thirty days of my life.

June 3: Temp is up. Back on cooling bed. Back
brace hurting Bret. Waiting and praying again.

Amidst the storm to save my leg, the battle to save my life raged on. A ventilator, IVs, machines, monitors and feeding tubes were all working together to keep me alive. It was a race against the clock every hour to deal with another problem. The infection was a constant enemy threatening to take my life. The nurses worked to get the temperature down. They were juggling one problem on top of another. My lungs were failing, my kidneys did not work and my heart was getting weaker and weaker by the day.

"Can we just pray?" April asked everyone in the ICU waiting room. April had been through her own storms of life. She overdosed on drugs when she was fifteen when we lived in Rockford. Five years older than me, she took the role of keeping the family together during those difficult days of living in the ICU waiting room. They had been camped out for three weeks, eating, sleeping and living in the hospital. My family, some friends and family members of other patients in the ICU gathered in a circle, held hands and prayed.

"Last I heard the prayer chain was reaching as far as Canada and England!" Cindy said. She was a close friend from back home. We used to spend hours riding my motorcycle on warm summer nights, talking about life. Cindy was the first person I can remember who ever shared anything meaningful with me about God. I did not have faith then to see what she saw, but she did not give up on me. Cindy was always very special in my heart.

Mom quickly stepped into the waiting room. Her voice soft and worried, she broke into the discussions, "Bret's lungs are failing. They're worried about blood clots. They're rushing him in for a lung scope." Mom reached out to Jana. Seeing the dark circles around Mom's eyes from little sleep in the last three weeks, Jana hugged her wondering how much more she could take.

They took me to another surgical room. It was cold and bright. The lung scope was a routine procedure. I had already been through five major surgeries and countless other procedures, any of which normally took several weeks of recovery.

"Doctor," the nurse monitoring my blood pressure said, "his blood pressure is dropping."

"What?" Dr. Schultz demanded. "What's going on? What are his other vitals?"

Before anything more could be said, the heart monitor went flat.

"Beeeeeeeeeeeeee," the monitor sounded loudly.

"Quick! Get me the paddles!" Dr. Schultz ordered, "Now!" He yelled, "Clear!"

Everyone jumped back out of the way as he shocked my body with volts of electricity, jump-starting my weak heart.

"Beeeeeeeeeeeee." The sound of the monitor continued to pierce the air.

"Again!" he yelled, "Clear!"

He shocked me again. My body bounced off the table for the second time.

"Beep . . . Beep . . . Beep," sounded the monitor.

"Yes!" one of the surgical nurses yelled, "it's beating again!"

As the room settled down from the unfolding drama, Dr. Schultz put his hands on the surgical cart I was lying on. Leaning forward he dropped his head in quiet relief and said, "Can't anything be easy for this kid?"

> *June 4: Bret in for lung scope. Heart stopped again!*
> *Returned to us again. How much more will God*
> *put on this boy?*

The next morning Dr. Witzkie came into the room just as the nurse was taking off the bandages for another scrubbing, the fifth by that time. Examining the tissues, he pulled out a shiny silver scalpel that looked like a small butter knife. Without a word he started cutting off pieces of black tissue up and down the edges of the open flesh. Sweat began running down my face as I watched him, anticipating he would hit a "live" spot.

"Excuse me, doctor?" Mom said.

"Yes," Dr. Witkie replied as he continued cutting. To him it was nothing more than routine work.

"Doctor, can I talk to you outside of the room. Now!" she demanded, entirely unusual for her soft spoken nature.

Following her request, he walked outside the room with her. She scolded him, "I want to tell you this boy has feeling down there in his leg. He feels all of that. You can't just cut it off like it's a piece of meat."

Dr. Witzkie put his hand on her shoulder and said, "You're really tired. You just need some rest."

"I will rest when Bret is well," she argued.

Dr. Witzkie went back into the room, but Mom could not watch. He began to cut again. Within seconds I let out a scream. Dr. Witzkie quickly walked out of the room and over to Mom. He said in a surprised tone, "You were right! Bret has feeling in that leg."

They discovered I had what is known as "spotty sensation." The nerves that make the muscles move are not the same nerves that allow sensation. I was able to feel some areas of my legs, but I still could not move a muscle.

June 5: Bret feels left toes. Some sensation in right leg.

Chapter 4 - Scrubbings

Dr. Benson came in carrying a small plastic box with needles in it. He pulled out some of the needles.

I asked him, "What are you gonna do?"

With a smile he replied, "I'm going to see just how much you can feel."

He began poking me with the needles. I found his manner to be somewhat unusual. The doctors and nurses treated everything like just another day at the office, yet it was my body they were poking and prodding with sharp objects! I often daydreamed about poking them a time or two.

"Can you feel this?" he asked.

"Feel what?" I replied.

"I guess that means you can't feel anything there." He continued, "What about here, can you feel that?"

"I felt that one," I said. I was happy I could feel something. Anything!

It was hard to speak, even when I was excited. The respirator had been in my throat for so long that it had damaged my vocal cords. I had to literally yell just to be heard. It wore me out.

"How does it feel? Is it sharp or dull?" he asked.

"Well, I can feel it but it doesn't hurt," I said. I did not realize he had slowly pushed the pin into my left upper leg about a quarter of an inch. That would have caused serious pain to a person with normal sensation.

He continued to poke and prod my legs, asking if I could feel anything. In some areas I could feel, but in other areas I could not. There were not many areas where it felt sharp. Dr. Benson explained to me that I had a certain "grade level" sensation. He continued to explain the sensation, but all I wanted to talk about was walking.

"When am I gonna start walking?" I asked. I never once thought I may not walk again.

"You've been here for over a month now, Bret. Usually if you're going to get anything back, you would see that happen in the first few weeks of the injury." Dr. Benson explained, "You are not able to move anything below your waist yet. People with your kind of injury in most cases never walk again. They also need a catheter to urinate and must be on a bowel program." He continued, "Your level of injury also involves sexual function, which means you probably never will be able to have children. We'll need to see you move something pretty soon if you're going to ever walk again."

His words cut through me like a sword. He may as well have said I only had a week to live. I looked around the room for something, someone to help me. No one could. All the talk about my condition was usually done outside of my hearing. I had not heard those things from anyone before. My family wanted to protect me since I had so many other problems. I was usually heavily sedated or going through a surgery of some type and not in a position to be talking about it. I knew there was a problem because my legs did not move, but I never guessed it could be permanent, nor did I realize it involved any of the other things he talked about.

"I'm sorry, Bret," Dr. Benson tried to console me. He smiled and quietly left the room.

"What's he talking about?" I whispered, "No way! What's going on?" I was alone and angry. My thoughts continued, "He doesn't know what he's talking about. I'm gonna walk again!" I cried in my heart, "God! No! Help me!"

Up to that point all I cared about, what I hoped for the most, was living for my own pleasure so I could be happy. I always asked God to give me happiness. I didn't pray for riches or power or fame. I just wanted to be happy. I thought happiness came from winning and getting what I wanted. I accepted Jesus as my Lord and Savior a year before the accident. Now that commitment to Christ was being tested. Did I truly not give Him my whole heart? Living my life in a wheelchair, crippled and helpless, was out of the question. If I could not walk again, I did not want to live.

> *"Humble yourselves under the mighty hand of God,*
> *that He may exalt you at the proper time, casting all*
> *your anxiety on Him, because He cares for you."*
> *- 1 Peter 5:6-7*

* * *

The scrubbings were getting to me. It was like the Chinese water torture. In war times, the Chinese would lay a prisoner of war on his back and drip small drops of water onto the prisoner's forehead.

At first the prisoner was thinking, "This isn't so bad. I can handle this!" But after several hours the small drops of water became like lead balls. After a little while longer, the small drops of water seemed like huge boulders! Soon it became the anxious anticipation of the next drop of water that drove the prisoner crazy. That was the Chinese water torture.

They were like the Chinese water torture to me. I did not want to go through any more of those scrubbings. But they came faithfully every four hours and lasted twenty minutes ending with my bed sheets soaked in sweat. Each time I was faced with the doctors' advice to let the leg go since I would never walk anyway. I felt like that war prisoner who was told he should give the information they wanted to end the torture and pain. But I refused to give in. I still could not bear the thought of losing my leg, or worse yet, never walking again.

A week or so into the scrubbings, another new nurse came into my room. She was young and seemed very compassionate. I complained to her about how painful the scrubbings were. She had not taken care of me before, so she was not familiar with my leg treatments.

She began to slowly take the bandages off. When she got to the gauze packed in the holes in my leg, I saw her face turn white. Although she was a nurse, it was a terrible sight to see. She slowly pulled out all the gauze and began to scrub the leg. She scrubbed very lightly and ended quickly. I am still not sure if she did that for herself or for me.

Later that night at about two o'clock in the morning it was time for another scrubbing. I began to talk with her about how senseless it seemed to do the scrubbing every four hours. I tried to persuade her skip one. She quietly put the scrubbing supplies away and walked to the door.

Looking back at me before she quietly walked out the door, she said softly, "No one has to ever know. It'll be our secret."

I closed my eyes and let my head drop back against the pillow. I quietly rejoiced in my victory. I could not have been happier for that moment in time.

* * *

Even the simplest achievements were a major victory. I had been in the hospital lying in bed, hooked to machines keeping me alive for nearly a month. My body was wasting away more and more each day. My doctors wanted to get me out of bed at least for a few minutes a day to keep the blood flowing. They cranked up the head of my hospital bed, but I could only stand to be upright for a few minutes at a time. Within minutes I began to feel dizzy. I quickly felt the room closing in on me.

I panicked. "Put it down! Please, put it down!" I begged.

The nurse cranked the bed back down. I soaked up the feeling of relief as the panic slowly went away. Yet I began to feel ashamed. "How am I ever going to walk if I can't even sit up?" I thought to myself.

In all the athletic training, hard work-outs and sweat, I had never experienced anything like this. I just wanted to forget my problems. I could not face the road ahead of me. It was too long and too steep. I wanted to hide.

June 6: Bret on tilt bed today . . . No more non-family. Fever is up. Praying for a good night. Scared.

"Good morning, Bret!" Jeff, my physical therapist, said with a hint of excitement in his voice, "We're gonna try something new today."

He walked into my room pushing an odd-looking chair of some sort. It was an ugly light blue color with thick cushions on the seat and the back. There was a crank handle on the side.

He cranked it down flat and said, "What do ya think? We'll transfer ya over onto this thing and get ya sitting up for a bit?"

"No thanks," I muttered, irritated by his joyful attitude.

"I tried that yesterday. I couldn't even sit up in this dumb bed." I complained.

"Well, I've heard you're into sports, and you know what they say: no pain, no gain!" he countered.

I grumbled, "This is a little different."

Before I could argue anymore, Jeff and a few nurses grabbed hold of the sheets on the bed and slid me over. "What is this thing?" I cried. "It's too hard! It hurts. Please take me back!"

"It's called a surgical chair," Jeff answered with the tone of a motivational speaker. I was sure he had that kind of training in PT (Physical Training) school and he was doing his best to motivate me.

I continued to grumble in my mind, "I'll do it when I'm ready. Just let me be!" I thought.

He gave me little time to think. The next thing I knew he had the surgical chair cranked up so I was sitting almost straight up. The room began to spin and close in on me again! I began to panic and yelled, "Put me down! I'm not ready!"

"You're never gonna be ready if you're not willing to feel the pain," Jeff replied.

I said angrily in my mind, "Pain! You don't have a clue!"

"It's gonna take some getting used to, but you can do it!" he challenged, "Come on, I've heard how tough and strong you are, let's see it!"

I sat in that chair with the room spinning around and around. I felt like I was dying! My back was on fire. I had never felt such pain. I wanted to scream, but Jeff was there. I gritted my teeth tightly and held my breath. Then I let out a long breath and began taking short breaths like I did when I used to lift weights. I remembered the training technique of fixing my eyes on some object off in the distance. I locked my eyes on a stuffed bear with balloons that someone had set on the table over by the door.

It seemed like I had been sitting there for hours. I was sweating. Then Jeff exclaimed, "Hey! Great job. You've gone one minute. Think you can go longer?"

"One minute?" I cried, thinking for sure his watch was broken. I wished I was dead. It seemed every cell in my body was crying out in pain. I was hearing a loud noise and the room seemed to be moving very fast now. I felt like I was about to pass out.

After a few more seconds, he let me back down and it was over. I could not bear the thought of doing it again.

> *June 7: Praise God!! Bret sat up in surgical chair today. I'm so excited!! Hope for good night.*

I dropped from 175 pounds to 120 pounds during my first month in the hospital. I watched as my legs dwindled down to nothing. I could not believe my eyes. They looked like skin wrapped around bones. I simply could not believe I was going through this.

I tried to move my legs when no one else was around. I concentrated hard to make my legs move. I looked at my toes for what seemed like hours and told them to move. I did not understand why they would not move. It was similar to trying to tell my nose to scratch my ear. I could think about it. I pictured doing it in my mind, but nothing happened.

My mind constantly went back to what I was like before the accident. I lived in "those days" because the present days were horrible. I felt cheated that I had lost everything I cared about. I felt like it was a bad dream and I wanted to wake up.

> *June 8: Bret's nervous about working on foot. Temp is good. Hope infection has been found. Bret resting, I hope. He misses his Bible. I hope I can help. Waiting and praying.*

The scrubbings continued.

A new doctor I had not met before came in to see me. He introduced himself as Dr. Cho. He spoke with a strong Korean accent in broken English. I could hardly understand him.

"Hello. My name is Dr. Cho," he said. "I am going to check your legs."

He poked and prodded me with needles like Dr. Benson had done. After he finished poking me with the needles, he slowly, quietly put them away.

"Are you gonna help me walk again?" I quietly asked, hopeful he could help me.

He looked down at me and in his broken English said, "I think you never walk again." He continued to explain, "Maybe use braces on legs. You try to walk with crutches. Maybe then you walk little bit for exercise. But no more."

I could not believe he was telling me that. Although I had never met him before, he just walked in, poked me a few times, and delivered his devastating news. Of course, it was no secret to all the doctors and nurses that I was never going to walk again. They were just doing their job and trying to help me face reality. But to me it was cruel.

Each new doctor or physical therapist that came into my room was my chance for some good news. I was grasping for someone, anyone, to give me hope. I thought maybe, just maybe, this person would be the one. But God made me look to Him alone.

People spend most of their lives gaining their self-esteem and identity in what they do or from their accomplishments. I spent most of my life building it on a foundation of sand such as athletic achievement and popularity. God was removing the very part of me that kept me from Him. My physical strength and physical control kept me from God. Just as the doctor cut away the dead tissue from my infected leg, God was cutting out the bad stuff I had spent years building. Infection was killing the flesh in my leg, just as pride and self-centeredness were killing the Spirit's work in my life. He was cutting out the "self" from my "self-esteem" and putting Himself in its place. I could no longer rely on myself, or others. I needed Christ.

One night a few weeks before the accident, Bruce and I were hanging out after a Bible study. We were in his dorm room together. It was just the two of us and we decided to pray. As we prayed, Bruce began by saying, "Lord, please make me the person You want me to be. Use me, Lord, for Your kingdom. Mold me and shape me to do Your work. Do whatever it takes to make me the man You want me to be."

I followed his lead and prayed the same thing. We agreed that we wanted God to use us, to mold us like clay so we could be His servants.

> *"Like the clay in the potter's hand,*
> *so are you in My hand."*
> - *Jeremiah 18:6*

Yet as I prayed that prayer, I wanted to take back the words as they were coming out of my mouth. I was scared what would happen. I did not yet know Christ well enough to trust Him completely.

Faith is the opposite of physical or mental control. As I lay in the hospital, I did not yet understand that. I did not understand that faith is trusting God more than myself. For the first time I was beginning to learn to trust in God. I had no choice. The doctors could not help me. The nurses could not help me. My family could not help me. Although God was using them to save my life, they could not offer what I really needed, which was to know and trust God.

June 9: Leg is really hurting now. Thank God there is feeling!

The pain was getting unbearable. Dr. Witzkie ordered a morphine pump, a small machine that holds the morphine that I could give to myself when I needed more pain relief. When I hit the button, it released a shot of morphine into my veins. The drugs sent me to a nice place away from the pain for a while.

As the scrubbings continued, I fought to survive them. I literally lived hour by hour waiting for the next scrubbing, hoping and praying the nurses would get too busy and forget the next one. I was preoccupied by the memory of the last scrubbing, not able to get it out of my mind.

I tried my best to have a good attitude even during the toughest times. Many people came to visit. I tried to put on a good show for them by acting like I was doing great. But Mom saw the real me. She saw the person inside of me crying and screaming to get out of the broken body. I hated it and I vented that towards her. After everyone left and it was just me and her, I let it all go. I cried, I yelled, I blamed her for the smallest problems that she had nothing to do with. She was my outlet. Yet she took the abuse and continued to love me through it.

Mom was raised by her Granny and Pop (her grandparents) because her dad ran out on them, and her mom remarried a man who didn't want her. Mom used to work at a cafe in her small town of Naylor, Missouri. Her dad would often come into the café, yet he did not even acknowledge her. I could never understand Mom's unconditional love.

June 10: Bret emotional when I got back. Can't be away. Not much progress on chair because of brace. Bret scared at night.

Nighttime was the worst. I felt the presence of evil in the darkness. I was scared of the unknown more than anything. It was the struggle between fear and faith. I was in the beginning stages of learning how to work out my fears through faith.

It seemed like a whirlwind. The medical people were telling me to face reality, but I felt God telling me to trust Him. When I listened to the world, I panicked. The storm raged on and on. It felt like I was on a small ship in the midst of a raging storm being tossed around by the waves. But when I trusted God and put my faith in Him, it was like finding the eye in the storm.

I longed for that peace, the eye of the storm. Amidst all of the pain and problems, I found myself retreating into a quiet and peaceful place with God where I found relief from the storm. I found that place often. It was safe. It was warm. It was wonderful. It was an amazing place. There were no pain, problems or trouble there. I discovered that this place was complete dependence on God. It was utter surrender to Him and His will. When my world was falling in around me, and when nothing could offer relief from the storm, I surrendered. I finally gave up my personal agenda, my desire.

After fighting hard and long, I finally turned to God and said, "Lord, I am yours. Your will, not mine, be done."

> *"In Me you may have peace. In the world you have tribulation, but take courage; I have overcome the world."*
> *- John 16:33*

Then I could breathe again. I entered into my safe place of peace with God and hid myself from the pain of the world around me. I loved it there. But I could not seem to stay there. I lost the connection with that amazing place and found myself back in the cold, cruel world of pain.

June 12: Really bad night. Talked to Doc. More morphine for scrubbings. Don and I are feeling lost and helpless.

* * *

"Joanie," Dad said as he and Mom sat in the ICU waiting room, "what are we going to tell Bret?"

"I don't know," Mom replied. "He thinks they're working to save his leg. That's what the scrubbings are supposed to do."

Dad continued, "Well, one thing is for sure, we can't tell him they're talking amputation again. That would be too much for him. He thinks he's gonna be walking out of here soon."

"Yeah, I know. But we have to be honest with him. We can't build him up with false hope," Mom said as she leaned back in the chair and sighed heavily, "What are we gonna do?"

They continued talking as Jana, David and April walked in. "So where are we at?" April asked.

Mom replied, "They're talking about amputation again."

"I thought we were past that!" Jana cried. "Why are they putting him through those scrubbings then?"

"We need to pray," April said calmly.

They all grabbed hands as they made a circle. Dad walked out as he usually did when they prayed. This battle was hitting everyone, each in a different place. They knew for me it was as important as life itself. Losing my leg meant there was no going back. It would be the loss of hope for a full recovery.

"Oh, excuse me," Dr. Witzkie said as he walked in.

"Doctor, what is going on?" Mom said. "Bret's nurse just told me you were telling her it's probably time to amputate."

"Yes, that's what I'm here for," he answered. "We need to talk."

"What's there to talk about. I thought we've already been through this," Mom said.

"Well, yes, we have. But now we're not so sure Bret has a choice," he explained. "The major arteries supplying blood to the lower leg are blocked off just above the knee. We need to do an angiogram to see if he has enough blood flow to do the grafting surgeries. His leg should be clean enough in a week or so to do that." He continued, "It is hard to say this, but the reality of the situation is that we've had several doctors look at Bret's legs and spinal injury. They're all telling us he will never walk again anyway. If we amputate, he could be home soon, and to a good place for rehabilitation so he can learn how to live in a wheelchair. I'm sorry, but I'm afraid that's where we're headed."

June 12: Doctor talking amputation again and no walking! Praying again. All the time!

It was late and my room was quiet. I could hear the low, constant hum of the motor on the air-bed keeping me afloat. The beep of the heart monitor broke through the silence as I wondered what they were talking about. Dr. Witzkie left quite awhile ago.

Minutes later, Mom and Dad walked in with Chaplain Oakland. I liked him, and he was helpful. As one of the chaplains on staff with the hospital, he came to visit often, but especially when things got really bad.

"Bret, we were talking with Dr. Witzkie," Mom said.

I held my breath. I sensed it was going to be bad.

"Son, you're leg is not getting better, even with the scrubbings," Dad followed. He paused, let out a breath as if he had been holding it, and continued, "They all say. . . Well, it's the doctors, they just don't think you'll be able to. . ."

"I know! They don't think I'll ever walk again, so why not cut the leg off and get it over with!" I argued, feeling the room close in on me. In an instant, my heart was pounding hard. I felt an overwhelming fear that I could not get a grip on. It felt like I was

46

falling into a dark hole and I could do nothing to stop it. Everything suddenly turned to slow motion. It did not seem real. It felt like a dream.

I wanted my old life back. My plan was to get out of the hospital in a few months. I planned to be back home running, jumping, playing summer league baseball, water skiing, and having fun before the next college year. They were telling me things that did not fit my plans. Nothing I did or said seemed to be helping. I could not get them to see it my way. I was losing control.

"Bret, it's going to be okay," Chaplain Oakland's gentle voice interrupted my panicked thoughts, "Our Lord is right here with us."

"But they won't help me!" I strained to say.

"Bret, they are helping you. They're just not saying what you want to hear," he replied with assurance. "Life is like that sometimes. You have to trust that God knows what He's doing."

"I do trust God. But they are not with me. They're all against me!" I cried. "They want to cut off my leg. They don't want to help me walk again," I protested with a raspy voice.

I was forced to face a decision that would affect the rest of my life. My leg was dying and it could very likely take the rest of me with it. Yet, I could not see past my old life. I could not see living life without my leg.

June 12: Help us Lord. Docs are negative about movement. Bret is panic stricken. Pushing for amputation. No!!

Chapter 5 – Fighting Hard

My mind raced with fear. I could not answer him. My stomach grew sick.

"I have to answer!" I worried.

I was beginning to slip into a coma-like state. My eyes rolled back into my head and my mouth dropped open. I could not move a muscle or say a word. I was totally and completely paralyzed. Dad stood above me talking, but I could not respond. Growing up I learned through strict discipline to answer respectfully when Dad spoke. But this time I could not say a word. I heard everything he was saying. I was able to think clearly as it was all happening, but I could not answer. Not a single muscle moved from the top of my head to the bottom of my feet.

I came out of it as quickly as it started. "Yeah, I can feel that," I answered with much relief. Dad was always testing me. He often stood beside the bed talking to me while touching certain areas of my legs without telling me he was doing it. Sometimes I felt it, other times I did not. It became a game of sorts.

"How about this? Anything there?" he asked again as he scraped the bottom of my foot.

It hit again. I could not answer. This time it was for good.

"Hey?" he demanded playfully, "What about this? Can you feel it here?"

Still not able to answer, I was scared again. Finally, he noticed I was not responding. He walked out. I thought for sure he was mad, thinking I was disrespecting him. I did not even give it a thought that I could not move. My only concern at the time was that I could not answer my father when he spoke.

Dad came back with a team of doctors and nurses. They quickly filled the room moving around me trying to figure out what was happening.

"Bret! Bret! Can you hear me?" a nurse yelled into my face. "Try to squeeze my hand," she continued. "Can you blink? Anything. Just give us a sign!"

I could not see them, but I knew Mom and Dad were standing off to the side watching. I tried to give them a sign to show them I was okay, but I could not move. Then I began to worry that I was not okay. I stopped worrying about not being able to answer Dad and began to realize it must be serious. Fear began to rise up in me.

Doctor Grahm, one of my surgeons, came beside the bed. He bent over close to my ear and said, "Bret, if you can hear me, you're going to be okay. You've had an allergic reaction to the drugs. You'll be okay in a little while after the drug wears off."

I was relieved to hear it would not last. I started to wonder how long it would take to come out of it because my mouth was dry. I wanted some water, but no one knew. I still could not say a word. There was no way to communicate my simple need.

Dad stood by the wall as he watched everyone leave the room. After they were gone, he was alone with me. He slowly took off the cowboy hat he always wore.

Bending over the top of me he whispered in my ear, "I love you, son."

A flood of relief came over me and I felt a huge weight lift. I had never heard him say those words before in my life. For just a moment in time the world seemed to stop. Everything around me became quiet and still. All of a sudden it was all worth it. The tubes, the machines keeping me alive, the injuries, the pain and even the paralysis were worth it for just a moment to hear those words.

All I knew in that instant of time was that my Dad just told me he loved me. Somehow that made it all okay. Dad lost his own father when he was ten years old. He was left to raise himself while his mother pursued other interests. He never had anyone teach him how to love, or show him how to be a father. Although he was a good father in many ways, showing affection was a sign of weakness to him.

Ten hours later Jane, a middle-aged nurse, was checking my vital signs when my eyes finally blinked. I had the urge to speak, but was not sure if I could. I tried. "Can I have a glass of water?" I asked quietly.

"Bret?" she replied with excitement, "Was that you? Say that again."

"Can I have a glass of water? I'm really thirsty," I replied.

Within minutes I had my glass of water along with several nurses and a host of family visitors. The room was packed full. Everyone was excited I was past another tragedy amidst the even larger one.

There were so many emotions, from fear to joy, panic to peace. None of it made sense. It was as if I were living a dream, watching from the outside and looking into my life as it played out those early days in the hospital.

* * *

"How's Bret doing? Is he walking yet?" someone asked.

Dad was at home trying to handle some business matters at the bar. He was bombarded with questions. "No. He cannot even sit up in a chair yet," Dad replied with a sigh.

"Can he feel his legs?" the questions continued.

The bar was a dark place, like most other bars. It was a place where people went to hide from their worries, stresses and problems. Hiding places are best in the dark where no one can find you. Although my parents kept it clean and nice, the smell of smoke and alcohol was thick as you entered. To some it was the smell of pleasure, to others it was the smell of death.

I hated that smell. To me it was the smell of ruined lives, people leaving their families behind to seek their pleasures and hide from responsibilities. For years I saw many very good hard-working people go from bad to worse as the alcohol destroyed them. Now the paralysis and infection were trying to destroy me.

June 13: Really bad night. His fight is back for now. How much longer can Bret hang on? He needs some good news. Praying again.

I was losing the battle. The scrubbings were taking their toll. I could not stand the sight of my weak and lifeless legs, nor could I stand to hear what the doctors were saying. I could not bear the thought of life in a wheelchair. I wanted a quick fix. I wanted out.

Drugs! The morphine was becoming my close companion. I was flat on my back hour after hour. The pain went from a deep ache to a burning pain. Bed sores were developing on my body from the pressure of lying in one position all of the time. The IVs, tubes and machines hooked to me kept me from rolling onto my side to relieve the pressure.

I hit the morphine pump button again. The pain throughout my body slowly drifted away. It was like jumping into a cool pool of water on a hot summer day. What relief! It was much like my place of peace I found with God. But soon the pain was back stronger than before. It came on quickly like a lion pouncing on its prey. I tried to hit the button again to make it go away. I longed for that relief. I waited. I waited some more. And I waited more. I hit the button again and again. Nothing. There was no relief.

I called for the nurses. "Ma'am, I think this thing is broke. It's not helping with the pain anymore," I complained.

Judy, a middle-aged lady, treated her job and me like products on an assembly line in a factory. She looked at the morphine pump machine and messed with it. Then in a sarcastic voice she said, "Well, there's nothing wrong with this. It only lets you have ten shots of morphine per hour. This thing recorded you've hit the button forty-four times! There's nothing wrong with this machine. The problem is you are turning into a drug addict!"

Those words sank deep. I had never allowed myself to get into drinking much, and I never touched drugs. I watched for years as I grew up how alcohol and drugs destroyed the lives of those I cared about. Growing up in the bar, I saw person after person throw away his or her life for another drink. I wanted nothing to do with any of that.

I felt embarrassed because I wanted the morphine. It took all my cares away whenever I hit that wonderful little button. It bothered me that I liked the drugs.

I discovered why drug addicts love their drugs more than anything or anyone.

I wanted to defend my addiction, my right to be rid of the pain that was so unfair. But the idea that I was falling in love with the pain drugs bothered me even more than the pain itself. I got scared. I had heard of war veterans who turn into drug addicts to escape the pain of their injuries.

I decided not to take any more pain medication. The doctors said I was crazy. I did not take anything more than Tylenol after that.

June 16: Bret won't take morphine.

* * *

Everyone agreed I was in denial.

"I'm gonna walk again!" I declared with confidence, yet my voice was still little more than a whisper from the damage caused by the respirator. "Let's do range of motion again," I asked, barely able to lift my head off the pillow as I struggled to fight back.

Range of motion was an exercise my physical therapist, Jeff, taught us to do. Whoever was helping me, usually Dad, would pick up my limp leg and move it up and down, back and forth. The idea behind the exercise was to train the muscles to work again while at the same time keeping them stretched and limber.

During my years growing up, Dad always pushed me to work hard as an athlete. He pushed me to run faster and grow stronger. Whenever visitors came to our house, he loved showing off his son's athletic abilities.

"Bret, come in here and give me twenty handstand push-ups," he'd holler from another room. When I finished, he'd bark out another request for fifty push-ups. I knew the fifty would quickly turn into one hundred as he pushed me to exceed the limits.

It seemed Dad was naturally the one to work with me the most on range of motion. How hard it must have been for him, who had little tolerance for physical weakness, to pick up my lifeless legs and move them for me. I strained to lift, pull, bend and push my legs as he moved them for me.

With each movement I asked anxiously, "Anything? Did you feel anything?"

"No, nothing yet," he replied.

Range of motion and more range of motion. After working and sweating without so much as a muscle flicker, I rested for a while. But I could not stop. I felt guilty when I was not working at it. I could not give up. I could not quit.

June 19: Please Lord, help us all. Bret really working hard on physical therapy.

When the pit can get no deeper, God sends a ray of light to give hope. My room was on the sixth floor of the hospital, the orthopedic floor. It was a double room, but I was the only patient in that room due to the special air bed I was on and all the machines and equipment necessary for my care.

I was looking out the window focusing on the green trees off in the distance as Dad and I were going through the daily routine of range of motion. I was lying on my back with Dad standing next to the bed. He was lifting my legs up and down, back and forth.

"It's been twenty minutes, how much longer do you want to go?" he asked.

"Are your arms getting tired?" I replied.

Not wanting to admit it he said, "Not a bit! I can go as long as you want." We continued, up and down, back and forth for a few more minutes. My focus was on the trees in the distance when Dad's voice broke through my solitude.

"Hey! It moved! I felt it move!" Dad cried out with excitement.

"What moved? Where? What are you talking about?" I demanded.

"Your leg, under the knee. It's your left leg. It moved. I felt it move," he nearly shouted.

"Let's try it again. Lift it up again!" I begged.

As he lifted my leg again, I pulled with all I had. There was excitement in the air and I felt a renewed strength. I had been waiting for this like nothing else in my life.

"Yes, it moved again!" Dad cried out, "It's moving!"

You would have thought we all won a multi-million-dollar lottery. Yet, it was just a flicker of movement in a single muscle. But it was more than that. It was the first movement after being told there was little or no hope. It was like a glimmer of light in my deep dark hole.

June 22: Bret had movement!! He is really psyched.
Praying again all the time.

Dr. Benson walked in early the next morning. He said with his usual upbeat tone, "What's this I hear your legs are moving?"

"Yeah!" I said with excitement, "I was doing range of motion yesterday and something moved under my left knee."

"How about these toes. Any movement there yet?" he asked.

"No," I answered, "just under the knee."

I paused. "When do you think I'll be up walking?" I asked.

Dr. Benson was wearing his bright white coat that doctors wear. He moved closer to my side and crossed his arms across his chest as he looked down at me. "I don't know. That movement could be all you ever get," he said without any emotion, as if it were just another day at the office. I was stunned. It was a constant battle, day by day, listening to what the medical people were telling me. I fought in my mind to believe God really was in control.

A few minutes after Dr. Benson left, Chaplain Oakland came in. He seemed to have a bounce in his step as he walked towards my bed. He sounded excited as he walked closer to my bed, "I hear there's good news in this part of the hospital. Everyone's talking about it!"

"Yeah, my left leg moved yesterday," I replied quietly as he walked in.

"That's what I hear! Ya know, you're the big talk in the hospital again. If it's not one thing with you, it's another!" he replied with excitement in his voice.

"But the doctors are saying it doesn't mean I'll walk," I said with a defeated tone in my voice.

"Yes, Bret, that may be true. But, then again, it may not be. We have to rely on God, not man," he replied in his usual wisdom.

"Yeah, I guess so," I sighed as I dropped my head back onto the pillow, comforted somewhat by his words of hope.

* * *

As in war, there is not much time to rejoice after a victory. So it was with my tragedy. There was little time to rejoice after my victory in getting a small bit of movement. Reality hit again. We were quickly coming up on more tests to determine if my leg could be saved or not.

> *June 23: Bret has a hard day. I am shaking. Worried about tests!! Bret seems so lonely. He is tired. I am praying for good news on the angiogram. Please, Lord, help us all.*

It was about six o'clock. Dr. Witzkie came in during his usual morning hospital rounds. The nurse automatically began to unwrap the bandages and remove the gauze packed into my leg. After she finished, Dr. Witzkie lifted my leg high in the air so he could look closely into the gaping holes. He took the small shiny silver knife again and began to cut away the black flesh dangling lose around the edges. I winced each time, fearing he would hit another live spot.

He finished and said, "Today is the day we're going to do the angiogram. Your leg is looking pretty good. Now we just have to see if there's going to be enough blood flow to make it work."

June 25: Starting day with angiogram. Praying while waiting. This decides for the leg. It has just got to turn out. Bret has been through so much already.

Dr. Shultz was the first one to talk with me about the test results. The room was full of friends from back home. I normally spent the summer on the beach back home as a lifeguard watching over the small children swimming in the town lake. My friends always stopped by for a swim and a visit. This summer they had to come to the hospital for visits. There was always plenty of company.

"Hey, guys, can I ask you to step out into the waiting room for a minute?" Mom asked my visitors as Dr. Shultz laid out the test results on the table for us to look at.

After all the visitors left, he looked up from the papers with a serious look on his face and said, "I don't like the test results. There does not appear to be enough blood flow to make this work," he said with a heavy sigh. "Let's wait to see what Dr. Witzkie says."

June 25: Dr. S not happy on angiogram.

Dr. Shultz left and I was worried again. The doctors held the keys to my future. I hung on their every word. When I realized he did not like what he saw in the angiogram, my hopes were instantly gone. If it were up to him, my leg was going to go. I wanted to run but quickly realized I could not move even if I wanted to. I felt so helpless. It seemed like it took days for Dr. Witzkie to show up. I agonized while we waited. He was supposed to be right over, but had been called to an emergency surgery.

Finally he walked in with two nurses and one of the residents. He clipped an x-ray up on a light screen. Walking over to the table with the angiogram test results, he stopped to look them over.

I watched him closely, wondering what he was going to say. This was it. I thought, "It all comes down to this. One man, and he gets to decide my whole future."

I prayed, "Lord, give him wisdom. Let this work. Let me keep my leg!"

I opened my eyes and he was still looking at the test results on the table, occasionally glancing up at the x-ray. He said something to his resident and the nurses, but I could not hear them. I saw the resident nodding as if he agreed with the doctor. I strained to hear them.

Mom was standing next to me holding my arm. I could feel her squeeze as the tension built. I wanted to be strong for her. I grabbed her hand to hear the news.

"Well, it doesn't look too good," Dr. Witzkie said as he walked over to the bed.

"There are small veins on the side. They look like they are taking over pretty good, but I don't know that it's going to be enough," he continued. "I just don't know."

He looked again at the papers on the table and glanced at the x-ray deep in thought. This was not just his normal case. He was breaking new ground. The surgery had never been done before in the Midwest. He had never done it before, himself. Worse yet, my heart and my blood flow made it even more risky.

Looking up from the table, Dr. Witzkie looked deep into my eyes. I locked onto his eyes begging for help, looking for hope. We connected. I felt like we were the only ones on the planet.

After a long pause he said, "I'm in if you are, Bret." He straightened his back and shoulders and continued, "Your heart is weak... your blood flow is minimal. But I think we can do it."

I could hardly believe my ears! All the scrubbings, the pain, the fear, the agony! It was all worth it!

"Yes!" I yelled with a scratchy voice feeling all the anxiety wash away.

Mom hugged Dad and Jana jumped in. It was as if we could all breathe after a month-long suspense. We started this journey nearly a month earlier. A journey that took me to the depths of my soul and theirs, but now it had brought all of us to the highest mountaintop!

Dr. Witzkie looked at me and watched my family. He smiled. It was a smile like I had not seen from him before. I could tell he was in this battle with me. He wanted to save my leg as much as I did now. We were headed into this together, arm in arm, as if partners fighting against all odds together. There is strength in numbers.

June 25: Dr. Witzkie says it's a go on the leg surgery. All systems go. Praise God!

Chapter 6 — Rain & Rainbows

Dr. Witzkie was about to cut a large muscle out of my back and graft it into the open areas in my leg where they had scrubbed for the past thirty days. The decision was made to save my leg, but everyone knew all too well it could mean losing my life. Dr. Witzkie began the surgery by making a long U-shaped incision under my arm. He cut me open from under my armpit, down to my waist and curved back up to the shoulder blade. He opened up the flesh exposing the large latissimus dorsi muscle in my back. He carefully dissected the muscle away from the other muscles, fibers, tissues and bones in my back. Once the muscle was cut free, he placed it in a refrigerator-like box to preserve it.

He then began to work on my leg cutting open further the areas that were already left open from the debrisment surgery, which had been scrubbed clean from infection. Now clean and pink, he prepared to graft in the muscle. The tiny blood vessels in my leg had to be spliced and made ready to be sown to the vessels in the donor muscle graft.

After four hours, the hardest part was about to come. By this time, they were not sure if they could continue. My heart had been fluctuating for the past four hours. The nurse in charge of the heart monitor was worried. After several more painstaking hours, the surgery was finally done. The muscle had been grafted into my leg and the blood flow seemed to be working, at least for now. My heart was beating on its own and maintaining a steady pace. The surgery was a success.

June 27: Bret went to surgery 7:30 am. Praying!!
Surgery took 8 hours. Working so far. Praise God!!
Now we wait until Monday.

I woke up from surgery feeling a burning pain under my arm where they took out the muscle. I looked down and saw my leg. It was ten times the normal size under the bandages. I wondered why it was so big. I was shivering cold and looked over to see Mom standing next to me. I was still on the surgical cart in the recovery room.

"Mom?" I asked, "Are they done yet?"

"Yes, honey. It took eight hours and it's all done. You made it through," she said softly.

"Do I still have my leg? Why's it so big?" I wanted to know.

I drifted back to sleep before she could respond.

I woke up later back in my room. There was a triangle bar above me to pull myself up. I reached up to grab it, and pain shot through my side and back where they cut me open. All that time and energy worrying about saving my leg, and I never once thought about losing the muscle in my back! For the first time, I realized there was a lasting price to pay for saving my leg.

The door opened and Karen, one of my nurses, walked in. She began checking the IV lines and working with the monitor. "I hear you've been through quite a time in surgery, but it went well," she said.

"Did it turn out okay? Can I keep my leg?" I asked.

"Dr. Witzkie says he won't know for a few days if the new muscle graft will attach itself," she explained.

"More waiting," I complained.

"Yeah, I guess so," she replied with a sigh.

It seemed like an eternity waiting through the weekend to see if the graft took hold and if the muscle was going to live. But that was not the end of it. If it worked, the following week I had to have a skin graft. Dr. Witzkie was going to take skin off my thighs and graft it over the new muscle. But he was not sure the skin graft would survive over the top of the muscle graft. We could only wait to see how things would turn out.

It was early in the morning. Dr. Witzkie walked into my room. The room and hallway were still dark. He came in with two nurses. It was quiet and I was alone. They began to unwrap the bandages. As they were doing that, Mom and Dad walked in. They hurried to my side and Mom grabbed my hand.

"We'll know in a minute," Dr. Witzkie said as he continued to remove layer after layer of bandage and gauze.

Finally he got down to the last layer. It looked like thick white foam that he cracked like an eggshell. It came apart in two large pieces as he peeled it off my leg. He pulled it apart and I could see my new leg. For the past month I watched the nurses scrub the exposed bone and tissues. Now it looked like a hunk of roast beef stuck to my ankle and a dark reddish layer of meat was stapled along the outside area covering the part that was left open. I saw hundreds of silver staples going up and down my leg and around my ankle.

I looked at my leg in amazement. My stomach sank. Just as I had not considered what it would be like to lose the muscle in my back, I had not thought of what my leg going to look like after the surgery. I was so consumed in the midst of the battle to save my leg that I never considered how my leg would end up after the surgery. I naively thought it would look like a normal leg. But it was hardly a normal leg.

I wanted to throw up when I realized my leg was now little more than a clubfoot. All the pain and fear and worry to save it, and I was left with something that would never be normal. As I looked at it, I tried to imagine how I was going to run and jump. My mind raced back into denial, and I could see myself running with my new leg. I pictured in my mind wearing a sock over it to cover up the scarring. That would turn out to be the least of my problems.

June 29: Doctor did dressing on leg. Looks great!
Praise God. Doing skin graft Tuesday maybe.

* * *

Mom peeked her head in the room and said softly, "Bret, you have a visitor."

She stepped around the door walking toward me. Her skin was bronzed from the summer sun and her hair was shoulder length blonde. It was Karie, the girl I dated all through high school. We broke up one year before the accident, because she wanted to get married and I wanted to finish school.

I tried to show my usual confidence as we greeted. "Hey, how's it going?" I said.

"Are you gonna be okay, Bret?" she asked softly as she tried to hide the shock of what she was seeing.

I was sure she had to be thinking how lucky she was to break up with me when she did. I was hardly a sight to see for a young girl looking for a husband. I was nothing but skin and bones, and white as the sheets.

"Yeah, I'm gonna get through this," I said, continuing, "They just fixed my leg and I'm gonna be up walking in no time. I get to go to a rehab hospital up in Minneapolis soon to get started walking again."

Trying to hide the doubt in her face, she forced a smile. I could tell she felt sorry for me. That hurt even more. We talked a little more and she left. I felt my hole get deeper as she walked out. It seemed like a cruel joke. I was paralyzed and fighting to survive. She was moving on with her life. Everything I had known and all that I wanted in life was being ripped away from me.

After she left, mom gave me the news that sent me deeper still into the hole.

"Did Karie tell you?" she asked.

"Tell me what?" I answered, unaware.

She's getting married next week," Mom replied. I could not respond. Now I was the one feeling sorry for myself. I thought for sure God hated me.

> *"For My thoughts are not your thoughts, neither your ways My ways," declares the Lord. "As the heavens are higher than the earth, so are My ways higher than your ways."*
>
> *- Isaiah 55:8-9*

June 30: Talked to Dr. Benson about back and pelvis. Healing good. Still won't say about walking. Karie came today. Victory for Bret. They are friends.

"Bret, are you okay with the news about Karie?" Mom asked.

"Oh, yeah! Sure. I'm happy for her. Our days are long gone and she needs to move on," I lied to Mom about my feelings. I knew it was hard enough for her, so I just acted like it was no big deal.

* * *

My world could not have gotten much worse. I needed a sign. I wanted to know God was real and that He had not forgotten me.

It was mid-July, eight weeks after the accident. In all that time, I had not been outside the hospital. I looked out the window. The sun was shining. I could see part of a brick building and a parking ramp where the helicopter sat. It was a beautiful summer day. I wanted to go out and feel the sunshine and smell the fresh air. I looked forward to the simple pleasure of seeing cars drive by and people walking on the sidewalk. I longed to see something that represented normal living.

"Can you take me outside?" I asked Karen, my nurse. "I have not been outside this place for two months. What do ya think?"

"Well, I don't know," she replied, "I'll have to check and see if it's okay." She left for awhile, but later came back with a recliner wheelchair. It was a special wheelchair that allowed me to sit up, but not all the way. I would still pass out if I sat up straight for too long.

"Does that mean I can go?" I asked.

"Yep. You're headed outside!" she said with a big smile.

Karen and Mom transferred me from the bed to the wheelchair. Soon we were headed towards the hallway. Out the door we went. Mom pushed me in the recliner wheelchair and Karen pulled along a dolly with the IV bottle and feeding tube machine.

I had not been out of the room other than on a surgical cart before that time. I was surprised to see how things looked from a different perspective, sitting up as opposed to lying down. They steered me past the nurses station, down the hallway to the elevators. I felt the excitement build. It was the first normal thing I had done for pure pleasure since this all started.

"Well, hello. Where's the party?" a lady in the elevator asked while we waited. She was wearing a nurse uniform, so I figured she worked there.

"Bret's been here for two months. He gets to go outside for the first time today!" Karen replied.

"Ding," the elevator sounded as we reached the first floor. The doors opened. I had not yet seen this part of the hospital. The lobby was large with beautiful large panes of glass on all sides. A beautiful open staircase wound its way upstairs to a balcony. People were moving in every direction.

My excitement grew as we moved through the lobby. The anticipation steadily built. I looked up again at the people walking by. It seemed so foreign. I had only been out of commission for a few months, yet it seemed like a lifetime. Our little outing was turning out to be more than I first thought.

We had only moved a few feet out of the elevator when we realized to our amazement that dark puffy clouds had moved in during our short ride down the elevator. It was dark outside. We could not believe our eyes. We moved a few steps closer and it began to pour down rain.

"What is this!" Karen exclaimed with surprise in her voice.

"I can't believe it," I declared with an angry tone.

"This is impossible!" Mom said as we walked closer.

Everyone in the lobby looked on with amazement.

Feeling rejected, Mom and Karen slowly turned me around and headed back toward the elevators. I felt like I just got hit with the final blow. I hung my head. It was a black eye on top of a black eye. God would not even give me something as simple as a stroll in the sun. I was sure He hated me now.

Thunder boomed loudly through the lobby silencing the crowd. The hard driving rain was all that could be heard. Only seconds passed by, but it seemed like an eternity as we moved toward the elevator. There was an eerie silence in the lobby.

At that moment someone yelled out breaking through the quiet, "Hey! It stopped raining!"

Heads quickly turned to look outside, and sure enough it stopped raining. The downpour ended as quickly as it began. There was a spontaneous gasp by everyone in the lobby. Mom and I looked at each other wondering what they were seeing. Mom shrugged her shoulders.

I looked at Karen and asked, "Can we go now?"

She nodded at Mom and they slowly turned me around toward the doorway. It was bright and sunny again. Mom pushed the wheelchair through the huge entrance doors and wheeled me around the curved sidewalk. The hot sun was shining down on us, and I felt its warmth deep into my bones. I smelled the fresh rain.

As we got further away from the doors I looked off to my right and there it was:

God's sign of hope! It was the biggest, most beautiful rainbow I had ever seen. I felt like I could reach out and touch it.

I felt a sense of warmth all over. It was not from the sun, but from the Son. A surge of energy went through me like I had never felt before. It was as if my Lord was standing right in front of me.

July 12: It rained and Bret saw a rainbow. God's sign!!

> " 'I know the plans I have for you,' declares the Lord,
> 'plans for good and not bad, plans for a future
> and a hope.' "
>
> *- Jeremiah 29:11*

My spirits were flying high after the rainbow. I thought about the meaning of the rainbow and it became clear to me. I realized the rain must come before the rainbow can shine.

* * *

Later that day back in my room, I heard a knock at the door. Before I could answer, she walked in. It was Marie Pletka. She was one visitor I hoped to see the most. Marie and I were in college together, and we dated the year before the accident.

"Hi!" Marie said with her usual happy tone as she walked into my room.

"Hey there! It's great to see ya," I replied with excitement, "You're looking great. You've been getting lots of sun!" Her skin was dark from the summer sun and she was prettier than ever.

Instantly I felt self-conscious. But that feeling quickly left as she made me forget I was hurt and could not walk. She did not seem to see my injuries. She looked at me the way she always used to. For a moment, it was almost as if the accident never happened. Seeing her helped me escape the hospital, the doctors, the nurses, all the bad news and the injuries. We talked, we joked and we had fun. I felt like the sun was shining again.

After Marie left, all I could think about is how I wished we could be together again. But just when I was beginning to catch my breath, the storm rolled in. Dr. Benson walked in with a spring in his step holding a large stainless steel drill with a long drill bit in it.

"What are you gonna do with that?" I asked with a sense of urgency in my voice as he came closer. By this time he was standing right next to me. He grabbed my leg and pulled the trigger. The high pitched whine of the drill gave me shivers.

Holding the drill high in the air, he replied, "We're gonna put this through your leg." Pointing to my leg just above the right knee he said, "Right here."

"Hey, wait!" I protested, "Aren't you going to put in any anesthesia?"

"Well, I suppose we can," He replied, seeming confused as to why I would ask such a question. "Would you like some?" he asked.

"Yes!" I proclaimed. "Can you explain why you are putting that thing through my leg anyway?"

"We're putting you in traction to pull your pelvis back in place," he said with a smile. My pelvis was broken in four places and was still crooked. They left it that way because there were too many other problems needing more immediate attention.

Dr. Benson gave me a shot to deaden the feeling in my leg. It was my right leg. I did not understand why they were putting it in that leg, since my right side was lower than the left. But they were the doctors, they should know. Minutes later Dr. Benson was holding the drill again. He put the tip of that long bit right up against my skin. He pressed the trigger on the drill a few times to rev it up. Then, without any warning, he drilled that long bit right through my leg.

"That oughtta do it," he said with satisfaction. "I've got to run, I'll stop back to check on ya tomorrow."

As he left, two orderlies and a nurse began hooking up weights, ropes and pulleys. They connected the pin to a rope and threaded it through a pulley above the foot of my bed. I watched as they put weights on the end of the rope. One of the orderlies let the weights drop down and it nearly pulled me off the bed. I grabbed the bars at the sides of the bed and hung on.

"You're not going to leave me like this, are you?" I said pleading with them.

They made a few adjustments and left me. I looked over to the doorway and could not believe they were already gone.

"Hey!" I yelled. "Help!"

I could not let go of the side bars to reach the nurses call button. I kept yelling for help. Finally, the door opened and it was Chaplain Oakland.

"Help!" I cried.

With a look of desperation, he ran over to the bed. "What's going on?" he asked, unsure of what to do.

"They left me like this!" I complained, "I can't let go. It'll pull me off the end of bed."

Chaplain Oakland hit the nurse call button and we waited together for a nurse to come in. He was standing at the head of my bed with his arms hooked under my arms holding me from being pulled off the bed. His head was close to mine. I was sweating. The nurse was not coming.

"Why?" I cried, "Why is this happening? It never ends! When is it going to end?" It had been over two months and it seemed like it was one bad thing after another. Wave after wave was hitting me with little time to take a breath. I wanted to see the rainbow again. I wanted this to be over.

"In Jesus' name. Say it with me," he directed, "In Jesus' name."

I said it with him softly. Tears rolled down my face, "In Jesus' name. . . In Jesus' name. . . In Jesus' name."

The storm was raging again, but I felt peace come to me by those words. We kept saying it together. I closed my eyes and kept saying it. I felt like I was in the eye of a hurricane. I could feel the storm raging, but I found my place of peace again.

After several minutes went by, one of my regular nurses, Judy, came in. I never liked her. I loved my other nurses and my doctors. The nurses were so kind, and the doctors did such a great job saving my life. But she was the kind of person that even when she was nice, I could tell she was faking it. She always made me feel like I had done something wrong. My peace left as soon as she walked in the door.

"Now what?" she demanded.

"We need some help here," Chaplain Oakland replied, still holding me by the arms. "This traction is pulling him off the bed."

"Well, it's not suppose to do that. I wouldn't think, anyway," she said in a sarcastic voice.

She called for the orderlies. When they arrived, they immediately went to work on the traction system. It turned out they forgot to set up the counterweight at the head of the bed. It was a good thing Chaplain Oakland came along when he did. He proved to be more than just a counterweight.

July 15: Traction for pelvic. Pin in leg. So much pain. Orderlies figure out better way. Bret wants to give up. Bret looks like Christ stretched out there.

The next morning Dr. Benson came in again. He was wearing a bright green and blue golf outfit. He had the same shiny drill with him again. I looked at the drill and wondered why he brought it with him. The orderlies who came with him began unhooking the traction system. Dr. Benson pulled out a needle and gave me a shot in the leg with the pin in it and the other leg too.

"What's going on?" I asked in my usual weak, raspy voice.

"We need to pull this pin out and put it in the other leg," he answered.

"What?" I demanded to know. "Why?" I cried. He didn't explain. He just smiled and connected the drill to the pin in my leg. Within seconds the pin was out. Then he put a new drill bit into the drill and moved over to the other leg. He grabbed my leg with one hand and touched the tip of the bit to my skin, just as he had done with the other leg. Without a word, he revved the drill a few times and drilled the new bit into the other leg.

I looked on in amazement, not believing my eyes. The orderlies quickly began to hook up the ropes, pulleys and weights again. This time they did not forget the counterweights.

Chapter 7 – Reality

It was the end of July, 1986, nearly three months after the accident. I had never been on a plane before, although I dreamed throughout high school of flying fighter jets in the Air Force. After ten weeks in the hospital, they sent me to a specialty care facility for spinal-injury patients. We were headed 250 miles by air ambulance northeast to Minneapolis, Minnesota, to a rehabilitation hospital called Sister Kenny Institute. I wanted to go there because they told us it was on the cutting edge of technology to help spinal-injury patients learn how to walk again. We were hoping for great things.

They unloaded me from the airplane into an ambulance. We arrived at a huge medical facility. I was wheeled in on a stretcher cart, because I got too dizzy riding upright in a wheelchair. It was a busy place. I was excited, yet scared. I had gotten used to the hospital in Sioux Falls and I felt safe there. I loved my doctors and nurses, and didn't want to change. But this was a new place, a new beginning.

July 22: Leave for rehab 12 noon. Go by Intensive Air. Said our goodbyes. We are here and they move fast here. Just got word, not out of woods yet for amputation. Bret emotional.

My new room was smaller and had one major difference. I had a roommate. His name was Dennis. He was from Huron, South Dakota, which was only twenty miles from my hometown of Woonsocket. His back was broken when he was driving a forklift and a box rolled off on top of him. His wife and two young children were in the room with him. I did not like the idea of having other people I did not know in my room, but I decided to make the best of it.

"Hi, I'm Bret. What's your names?" I asked politely.

They introduced themselves and we talked briefly about home since we were from the same area. It was not too long into the conversation when I announced that I planned to walk out of that place.

I said, "Yeah, I'm gonna walk again and I'm walkin outta here, that's for sure."

Dennis looked at me and quickly replied, "Me too! I'm walkin' again, man. I ain't sittin' in this chair the rest of my life."

Something in his face and eyes told me he did not believe his own words. I felt bad. I could also tell by the way his wife acted that she probably was not going to stick with him through it. That turned out to be true. She left him within a year.

The door opened and a nurse, Betty, came in. "Bret, I want you to meet some of the residents here," she said as she pushed in a young girl in a wheelchair. It was Kimmy!

"Kimmy! How are you?" I blurted out.

Kimmy smiled. She was a cute girl from Alpena, a town fifteen miles northwest of Woonsocket. They were our archrivals in sports, and although we were very competitive, we were all friends.

"Hey, Bret. It's good to see ya. Have they been good to ya?" Kimmy said with a sweet soft voice.

"It's great to see ya." I was feeling weird inside. I was happy to see her and to know she was alive, but I felt scared for her. She could not move her arms or legs. Kimmy was part of the reason we decided to come to Sister Kenny. She was hurt in a motorcycle accident a month before mine. We heard her neck was broken and that she was paralyzed, but we did not know how things turned out for her.

Seeing her helped me to feel like I was not alone in this new, busy place. As we were greeting each other, Betty locked Kimmy's wheelchair into place and stepped aside as another nurse wheeled a guy into the room, stopping him next to Kimmy.

"This is Alan," Betty said, introducing him.

"Hey, how's it goin?" I asked.

Alan sat in his wheelchair with a board lying across the armrests. His hands lay flat on the board. He could not move anything from the neck down. Alan and Kimmy were quadriplegics. That meant they lost the use of all four limbs, their arms and legs. Alan still had a halo on his head. It was a metal contraption that circled his head with bolts screwed through the ring and into his skull. He could only move his eyes and his mouth.

"Hey, what brings you here to the cities?" Alan remarked with a casual tone, which I learned distinguished him from most others. I was surprised, because it was like just another day for him. He did not seem too overtaken by his circumstances.

"A car turned in front of me and threw me into a tree," I replied.

"Oh, really?" Alan said, as if preparing to top my story. "I dove into a lake and broke my neck. Damn city! They should have had a sign warning people not to dive there."

I liked this guy. He did not mince words. He said it like it was. His directness was refreshing after months of people being extra careful not to say anything that might hurt my feelings. People never know what to say when they are visiting someone in such bad shape.

We talked for quite awhile. It was nice to visit with others who understood what I was going through. We were all in this together, which made for lasting friendships.

"Have either of you gotten any movement back yet?" I asked.

"Nope. Not a muscle below my neck. Haven't moved a thing since hitting the bottom of that lake," Alan said in his usual direct, sharp tone. Alan had a way of emphasizing his words that made conversation with him interesting.

Kimmy jumped in, "I can lift my arms, but I can't move my fingers," she explained as she demonstrated by slowly and awkwardly lifting her arms up toward her face. She had braces on her arms below the elbows extending to her fingers.

"What are the braces for?" I asked.

"They keep my fingers from locking into a fist," she answered, still moving her arms.

Continuing our show-and-tell, I said, "I can do this much." I pulled my leg up as I had been practicing for the past week.

"Hey, that's pretty good. Are they saying you're gonna walk?" Kimmy responded.

We all had fallen into the habit of hanging onto what "they", the doctors, said about our conditions.

"No, they're not sure. But I know I will," I replied with confidence. I wondered if Alan and Kimmy would ever walk again.

Early the next morning my new doctor came in. Her name was Dr. Day. She was a middle-aged gal. I liked her right away. She seemed nice. She was tall and thin with short black hair. She was wearing a white doctor's coat and carrying a clipboard.

"Bret, we're happy you're here with us. We are going to start you on physical therapy just as soon as we determine where we are at with the infection in your leg," she explained.

Dr. Day had a resident doctor with her who was not so nice. Her name was Dr. Hagger. I could tell from the start she was not going to be much help. There was something about how she looked at me. I did not see any compassion in her eyes. When she looked at me, I felt like she was angry.

"Bret," Dr. Day said with a kind voice, "this is Dr. Hagger. She is a resident physician working with me this summer. We hope you are settled in and feeling welcome here."

"When are we gonna start walking?" I asked. "All we've done so far is more tests."

I had imagined as soon as I arrived they would be working with me constantly. I pictured in my mind new technology with machines and mechanical devices that get people up and walking again.

Dr. Hagger interrupted, "Well, Bret, the first thing you need to know is that you will never walk again. You need to face reality and learn to live in a wheelchair. That is why you are here."

"What?" I demanded, "Mom! What is she talking about?"

Dr. Day quickly took Dr. Hagger by the arm and escorted her out of my room. Mom followed close behind. I did not see Dr. Hagger again after that.

July 27: Conference today. Three month stay. Bret doesn't even want to think of wheelchair long term. So much pain for Bret.

The next day they finally let me go to the physical therapy room. I saw it when we came in the very first day. It was a large room with exercise equipment, parallel bars, and mats on the floor. In a room off to the side, there were chairs in front of some sort of bicycle machine. Three people were sitting in these chairs. They each had electrical wires connected to their legs. I later learned these people were all paralyzed. A computer sent electrical impulses to their muscles connected by the wires. The electrical impulse made their muscles move so they could pedal the bicycle. A physical therapist in a white medical coat stood by a computer watching them while they all pedaled the bicycle machine. I could not wait to get in there and start working. I had visions of working out with weights, pedaling that computer bike and walking all over.

Back in my room, a young lady came in and introduced herself, "Hi. My name is Mary O. and I'll be taking care of you today."

"Hi Mary O. What's the 'O' part for?" I asked.

"My last name is O'Neil," she explained. "I go by Mary O. because there's another nurse on the floor by the name Mary. We call her Mary B."

"Sounds good to me," I said, "I hear I get to go to PT today. Are you taking me?"

"Yep, right after we get you fed and cleaned up," she answered.

I liked Mary O. She was nice looking with a wholesome look to her. I felt like I could trust her. I later found out she was a single mom with a little three-year-old daughter.

Mary O. transferred me onto a wheelchair. It was the first time I sat in a real wheelchair. It felt okay for the first minute or so, then the pain in my back began to burn deep inside. I wanted to lie down, but I was embarrassed to ask. Finally I could not hold it anymore.

"Mary O.?" I hesitated. "Can I lie back down?" I asked quietly as I fidgeted in pain sitting in the wheelchair.

"No," she replied firmly. "That's part of the physical therapy I hear you've been wanting so badly." She continued making the bed and did not even look back at me when she answered.

I was left with nothing to say. In my hopes to walk again, I failed to consider that it would involve more pain. Soon after, Mary O. got behind the wheelchair and began to push.

"Here we go," she said pushing me out of the room, "We're off to PT."

That helped take my mind off the pain. She wheeled me past several patient rooms, and I looked into each one wondering why the person was there. Each one had a tragic story. I felt excited as we got closer. Mary O. continued pushing the wheelchair around the corner and into the PT room. I couldn't wait to get started.

"I'll leave you here for now. Julie will come to get you when she's done with her other patient," Mary O. said.

I waited, wishing I could watch from my bed lying down. The pain in my back was getting unbearable even amidst the excitement of finally being in the PT room. I saw people doing all sorts of different exercises. My favorite was the parallel bars. I saw an older lady walking in them. I watched, imagining I was doing it. It seemed like I sat there forever.

Finally Julie came over to me. She was a younger girl with short blonde hair. She seemed upbeat and nice. "We're going to take you over to the pulleys and get your arms some exercise first, okay?" she explained.

"My arms?" I replied. "It's my legs that need the work," I remarked impatiently.

"I'm sure you'd like to try walking, but I have my orders."

Julie moved me over to a wall with pulleys and weights attached. She turned the wheelchair around so I was facing away from the wall. She quickly hooked up weights to the pulley and handed it to me.

"Now pull the handle forward and we'll see how much weight you can do," she instructed.

I pulled the weight forward without a struggle.

"There was nothing to that. Let's add some weight," she said.

I continued to pull the weights forward without any problem, and she continued to add weight until she could not add more to the pulley.

"Wow! You are strong," she remarked, "You've done this before, I can tell."

"Can we hit the parallel bars now?" I begged.

"I'm sorry, we can't. We have to work on occupational therapy now," she answered.

"What's that?" I asked.

"That's where we try to teach you how to navigate in the wheel-chair," she explained.

"What?" I argued. "There's nothing to it. I don't need to learn how to work this thing! I just need to get up and start walking again."

"I'm sorry. I'm not the doctor and I don't make the rules," she said calmly.

We went into a room that looked like a kitchen. It had a sink, countertops, a stove and a refrigerator. There was even food in the refrigerator.

"Now, I want you to maneuver your wheelchair over to the refrigerator, open the door, and get out the peanut butter. Think you can do that?" she asked sweetly.

I felt silly. "I came all the way from South Dakota to this high-tech rehab place to open a refrigerator door?" I complained.

Suddenly, I saw myself as an invalid learning how to live my life in a wheelchair. I became very angry. I was hurt. I was embarrassed. I wanted to die.

I angrily pushed myself over to the refrigerator and opened the door effortlessly as if I had been in a wheelchair all my life. I reached in for the peanut butter, pulled it out and set it on the counter top. Then I turned back, grabbed the refrigerator door and slammed it shut.

"Go tell the doctors I said, 'There's your peanut butter!'" I grumbled.

I left that sweet girl standing there in the make-believe kitchen as I pushed the wheelchair out and back to my room.

* * *

The infection was causing more problems. Dr. Day called in a specialist. He ran tests and decided more surgery was needed. Early the next morning they came to get me.

August 6: Bret out of surgery okay. Took off more
tissue. Left hole in heel. Some bone infection also.
Antibiotics for six weeks. Long time for healing.

After surgery, the new infection doctor, Dr. Smith, decided my veins were all used up from the IV's. He decided to go with a new way to pump antibiotics into my veins. It was called a Hickman catheter, which is a large tube inserted directly into the aorta of the heart.

I was prepped and taken into surgery again. The anesthesia doctor gave me drugs through an IV and I quickly drifted off to sleep. He did not give me enough of the drug, however, to put me completely out.

"Nurse, I need the scalpel again," I heard the doctor say.

His voice sounded far away. I did not know where I was or what was happening. In a cloud of hazy thoughts, I felt like I was dreaming. The surgery continued and I felt the doctor pulling at my chest. I heard voices, although they seemed muffled and far away. I felt more tugging at my chest.

Suddenly I woke up enough to realize we were still in surgery. "Hey!" I screamed, "I'm awake! Stop! Quit! I can feel it!"

The words went through my mind but could not go any further. I could not talk. I tried to tell them. I tried to move. But I was stuck in a half-conscious state, not able to communicate with them. I could hear things and I could see blurred objects and people, yet they did not know I was partially awake. I felt like I was dreaming but could not wake up.

I held my breath and waited. "What's going to happen?" I worried, "How much more are they gonna do before they realize I'm awake?"

The doctor was pushing and pulling on my chest. He complained to the nurses, "This catheter will not go in!" I heard him say adamantly.

Finally, I heard the doctor say it went in and it was time to sew me up. I waited for the needle. I could see him holding something up high. He was looking at it as if to measure it. I figured it had to be the needle. Then he reached down towards my chest. I felt the needle go into my skin and the suture material go through. The doctor pulled it tight and began to sew another stitch.

August 12: Waiting for Bret to come out of getting Hickman. It took longer. Had hard time getting it in. I was pretty worried. He is so tired and in pain.

Before the Accident

Merkle Named to 9A All-State Team

The seniors on this year's basketball team and cheerleading squad are back row Bret Merkle, Trent Steichen, Craig Runestad, Lee Regynski, and Dan Ball; Front row, Lisa Baysinger and Lori Olson.

Ace of the Week

☐ **BRET MERKLE** complete 7-of-14 passes, six of them for touchdowns, for total of 172 yards. Merkle threw scoring passes of 18, 20, 4, 50, 20 and 8 yards in Woosocket's 46-6 trouncing of Tulare.

Merkle's passing arm saves Redmen

WOONSOCKET — The passing arm of Bret Merkle proved a valuable asset for the Woonsocket Redmen Friday night as they rolled to a 28-8 non-conference victory over the Ramona Rockets

Newspaper picture of Bret's damaged motorcycle.

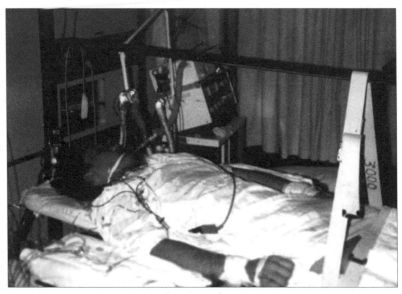

Bret clinging to life in ICU the first days after the accident.

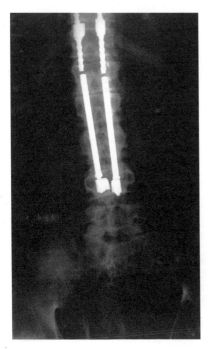

X-Rays of the Harrington Rods
stabilizing Bret's broken back. The
Rods have been broken, likely
through Bret's many adventures
trying to live a "normal" life.

Bret's Medical Records

NAME Bret Merkle   DATE 5-16-86   PHYS. GMB   4-4-65

~~Box 323~~

ADDRESS Woonsocket, S.D. 57385   AGE 21

RESPONSIBLE PARTY   INSURANCE CARRIER

EMPLOYER NOTIFIED   Father: Don

PRELIM. REPORT   FINAL REPORT

AREA CODE AND TELEPHONE NO.

Referred: DR. D. GRAHAM

5-15-86 - Patient seen in consultation at SVH after being involved in a motor-cycle accident on the 15th of May. IMPRESSION: 1) Fracture dislocation, L1-2 with incomplete paraplegia of lower extremities. 2) Multiple pelvic fractures, 3) Rule out intra-abdominal bleeding. 4) Sprain of right ankle, rule out frac-ture. DISCUSSION: Harrington rod with open reduction of the fracture dislo-cation at L1-2 is being scheduled. Will manage the pelvic fractures with bed rest and serial x-rays. Close observation of the ankle will also be obtained.
         GMB

5-16-86 - Patient underwent open reduction and internal fixation of fracture dislocation of L1-2 with application of Harrington distraction rod assisted by Dr. J. Johnson. He tolerated the procedure well. GMB No Post-op charge for office

7/28/86 DIAGNOSIS: FRACTURE DISLOCATION L1-2 WITH PARAPLEGIA only until 7-16-86

DRS. JOHNSON, BENSON & CARLSON

85

SIOUX VALLEY HOSPITAL

DISCHARGE SUMMARY

MERKLE, Bret
11/?-??5
Rm. 2109
Dr. Graham
Dr. Greg Schultz

Date Adm: __5-15-86__ Disch: _____   Date Dictated: __7-21-86__ Transcribed __7-21-86__

DISCHARGE DIAGNOSIS: 1. Traumatic rupture of descending thoracic aorta. 2. L1- L2 spine fracture dislocation. 3. Paraparesis secondary to L1-L2 spine fracture dislocation. 4. Malgaigne pelvic fracture. 5. Cellulitis involving the right foot and lower leg. 6. Complete heart block secondary to vagal reaction, resolved. 7. Occluded right popliteal artery. 8. High output congestive heart failure, resolved. 9. Left vocal cord paresis.

PROCEDURES: 1. Exploratory laparotomy. 2. Harrington rodding of spinal cord fracture dislocation. 3. Repair of traumatic rupture of descending thoracic aorta. 4. Bronchoscopy. 5. Right femoral arteriogram. 6. Right latisimus dorsi free flap to right lower extremity. 7. Split thickness skin graft to right lower extremity.

GS:crd
cc: Dr. Greg Schultz
    Dr. Graham
    Dr. Braithwaite
    Dr. G. Benson
    Dr. D. Witzke

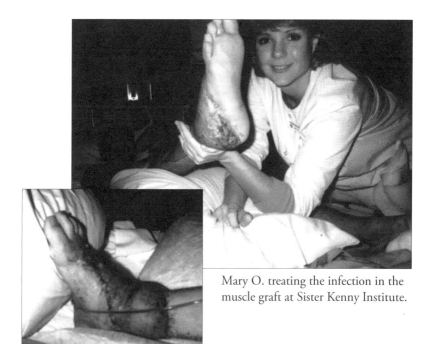

Mary O. treating the infection in the muscle graft at Sister Kenny Institute.

The muscle graft.

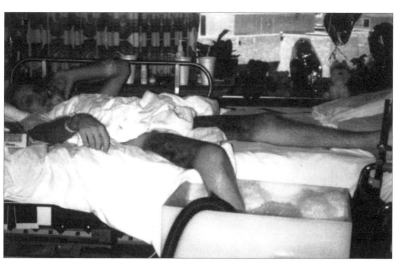

The new muscle graft is being cleaned by a medicated whirlpool bath and the skin graft is healing while Bret talks on the phone.

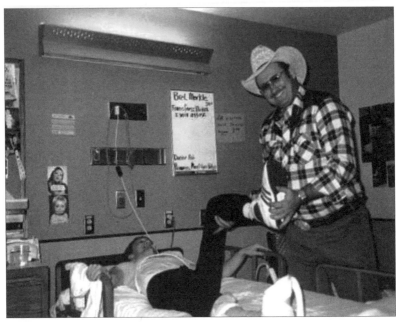

Bret's Dad helping with range of motion exercises.

The Paras and Quads, from L to R, Kenny, Bret, Dennis, Alan and Richard.

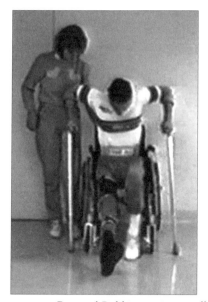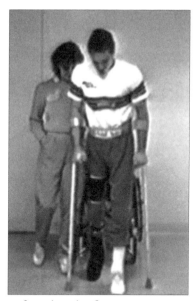

Bret and Bobbi practicing walking after taking his first steps.

WITH BEST FRIEND — One of Bret Merkle's best supporters through his ordeal has been high school friend, Jeff Jenssen, right.

(Photos by Cindy Larson)

Woonsocket man credits God, friends for his recovering

Bret and Dub working out in the high school gym.

Fun with the Family!

Left to Right: Hannah, Mary (our foster daughter), Sarah, Joshua, Angela, Ellie

Mom and Dad standing with Bret in the newly built law office on their ranch.

Living Life to the Fullest!

Riding Dan-Bar. Bret's legs tied to the stirrups.

Bret finally got a trophy buck.

More Wild Adventures!

VictoryWalk Ministries

Bret sharing God's power at an FCA rally.

Bret sharing with young men in a prison in Texas.

Bret leading a Bible study with men in a wood pallet and cardboard box community in Mexico.

Bret sharing God's love with boys in China.

Chapter 8 – Praise in the Storm

It was early in the morning, about seven o'clock. My least favorite nurse came into the room to do the morning rituals. I hated it. One of the worst things that goes along with a spinal injury is that a person is reduced to something less than human. One day you're perfectly healthy and normal, and the next you cannot even perform some of the most basic bodily functions. For me it was painful and humiliating. She turned me on my side and began her duties. I screamed in my head and wanted to die each time it happened.

"Why God?" I cried in my mind.

Enduring the shame and humiliation of what I was going through, tears slowly rolled down my cheeks. I slipped deeper and deeper into a depressed state. Just when I felt I could not slip further downward, I felt God speak. It was very clear. He gave me a picture. It was a picture of a word. The word was "Praise."

A few days earlier, Bruce's brother Maurice stopped for a visit. He brought his wife and two kids. He lived in Minneapolis and heard from Bruce that I was at Sister Kenny. Maurice gave me a book entitled, *Power in Praise*. It talked about the power that comes from praising God, especially during the darkest and most painful times in our life. The author, Merlin R. Carothers, explained:

> "God does have a perfect plan for your life and for mine. We may look at the circumstances surrounding us and think we've been standing still forever in one painful spot. The more we pray and cry for God to help us, the more the circumstances seem

97

to pile up. *The turning point cannot come until we begin to praise God for our situation instead of crying for Him to take it all away.*" (pg. 9)

> *"I will bless the Lord at all times;*
> *His praise shall continually be in my mouth."*
>
> *- Psalm 34:1*

Instantly when God gave me the picture of that word, I knew it was from Him. I felt like He gave me another rainbow to help me through the storm. Quietly, in my mind, I gave up complaining about the painful procedures, the miserable situation, and even the nurse I did not like. I replaced it all with praise for God.

"Lord, I don't know how to praise You right now. I just know I have to," I prayed.

"Lord Jesus, I praise You for who You are. I praise You that You are in control. I praise You for what I am going through. Lord, I know You love me. I praise You, Lord Jesus," I continued.

I felt peace amidst the storm. The pain slipped away and I entered His sweet presence.

As I prayed, I felt God's soft, strong presence say, "Bret, this must be for now. I am showing you things you need to learn. Trust Me."

Merlin R. Carothers continues,

"When we sincerely accept and thank God for a situation, believing that He has brought it about, there is released into that situation a supernatural, divine force that brings about changes beyond what can be explained as an unfolding of natural events." (pg. 12)

"If we want to be able to praise God in everything, we need to be sure our foundation is solid and without cracks of doubt and uncertainty." (pg. 20)

I would have gladly traded another six months of misery for one more minute of the peace I felt at that moment in His presence. Nothing can replace it nor compare to it.

Later that day I was back in the PT room. By this time, Dennis was back home and Alan moved into my room. We had gotten to be good friends. We were about the same age and had a lot in common. We often stayed up late into the night talking about anything and everything from cars to girls to sports. The conversation always seemed to steer towards God.

I learned that Alan was heavily into alcohol and drugs when he was injured. He grew up with an abusive father who drove him to such an escape. I loved talking with Alan because he was not afraid to talk about God. Alan did not have a personal relationship with Jesus, but he was interested in finding out more about Him. There was something about Alan that drew me to him as a friend, not just a hospital roommate.

I was sitting in the wheelchair waiting for my turn on the mat so I could roll around, supposedly to get some exercise. There was excitement in the room because Alan was about to try walking for the first time. He moved his toes a few days earlier. His legs began to move soon after. I watched Alan as he was about to stand up in the parallel bars. His therapist was holding onto a belt wrapped around his waist.

His therapist counted to three and pulled up on the belt. Alan slowly stood up in the parallel bars. He stood trying to balance while hanging onto the bars. Slowly he put a foot forward. Then he stepped forward with the other foot. He took another step and then another. Alan was walking!

I was so happy for him. He was actually doing it. But I quickly felt my joy for him turn to envy as I thought of myself. "Why can't that be me?" I cried to myself.

I watched Alan and his therapist as he continued to take slow steps. I was torn inside. I was happy for my new friend, but I fought with my feelings. I wanted to be in those parallel bars walking. I did not want to watch someone else get the chance of a lifetime, to walk again when all odds said otherwise. I sat in the wheelchair determined I was going to be doing the same soon.

* * *

The rehabilitation staff scheduled programs for us to get out of the hospital. One such event was taking us on outings. The outings were designed to help integrate us back into society as a "disabled" person. I could not accept that part of it, but I liked getting out of the hospital.

Each outing was different. We went to malls, movies, restaurants, and other social kinds of places or events. I could sit in a wheelchair by this time for a few hours, but only with a special cushion to ease the pain. One day they took us to a mall where we were supposed to maneuver our wheelchairs in and out of stores. People stared at us sitting in the wheelchairs. That made me very uncomfortable. I was self-conscious about it, even embarrassed.

Paraplegics and quadriplegics went on the trips. Those of us who still had use of our arms were affectionately called "Paras," and those who could not use either their arms or legs were called "Quads." The "Paras" were allowed to try something that I considered fun and challenging. For those who are crazy enough to try, a person can ride up and down an escalator in a wheelchair. Susan was our escort for the outings. She was a "Para" herself and used a sports wheelchair. She was really good at maneuvering it. Although I hated it, I enjoyed the challenge of doing tricks in it like she did.

Susan wheeled her chair up to the escalator and confidently jammed its wheels into the steps of the escalator. She quickly grabbed the black rubber side-rails of the escalator, and it instantly pulled her up as she sat in the chair. It looked pretty fun doing that.

I was riding in an old crate of a wheelchair because my leg was still wrapped and needed to be elevated. Instead of a cool sports wheelchair, I had to sit in that big old heavy crate. The legs on it could be cranked up so my right leg was elevated.

"Hey, Bill. Come over here so I can do that!" I yelled out at one of the therapists who went along on the outing.

"Well, okay, but you have to be very careful," he said as he walked over. "It's not as easy as Susan makes it look."

I saw him head over toward me. In my excitement to finally have a little fun, I went ahead without him. I jammed the old crate wheelchair wheels into the step of the escalator and grabbed the side rails. The escalator pulled me up.

"Hey, nothing too it!" I yelled to Bill as I looked back over my shoulder.

"Yooouuuu!" Bill hollered. "You were supposed to wait for me!" Bill hurried to catch up to me but he was too late. I was already close to the top. "Be careful! Hold on!" I heard him yell as I went higher and higher.

Getting closer to the top, I did not realize the danger that waited ahead. There was a small ledge at the top on the very last step. The wheels of the wheelchair needed to lift up and over the ledge or it would stop dead in its tracks, causing the person in the wheelchair to lunge forward out of the chair. On the other hand, if they let go of the rails, they would go tumbling backwards all the way to the bottom.

I reached the top of the escalator and sure enough, the front wheels of the old crate wheelchair got caught in the ledge. The wheels hit hard, bounced and jolted me forward. I hung onto the side rails with all I had. As I hung on, I felt myself being pulled further forward from the wheelchair. Instinctively, I knew if I let go I would tumble backwards. At the same time, I realized that if I held on any longer it would pull me out of the wheelchair and throw me onto the floor.

There was only a split second to make a decision.

"Bret! Hang on!" Bill's voice broke through my thoughts of survival that were swirling around in my head.

I had to do something to buy time for Bill to catch up to me. I knew there was only one thing I could do. I quickly let go of the side rails just long enough to fall backwards a few inches. As quickly as I let go, I grabbed the side rails again to keep from falling backwards any farther. As I clutched the side rails, I felt it jerk me forward, nearly pulling me out of the wheelchair. I let go again and quickly grabbed the side rails tightly to buy another second of time. Almost as quickly as I grabbed the side rail, it jerked me forward from the wheelchair. I let go and quickly grabbed them again. I continued to do that, falling backwards and jerking forward again and again.

Finally, I felt something behind me. Bill grabbed the handles on the back of the wheelchair and pushed down, lifting the front wheels off the ground. I felt myself tip back with my head slamming back against Bill's chest. The front wheels were lifted up and over the ledge. Bill pushed me off the escalator to safety.

"Please wait for me next time!" Bill scolded me as he pushed me to safety. "You could get hurt even worse if you're not careful!"

I felt the stares of many who had been watching. I did not want to appear to be a big fool so I quickly acted like it was all a big game.

"Come on, let's do it again!" I replied, not really wanting to.

"You're nuts!" Bill answered.

I liked that. It set me apart. I was not just another disabled person. It gave me some sort of identity; whether good or bad, it was something. I was now the crazy guy in the wheelchair. It did not seem as if I had learned much of a lesson from the accident.

Soon after the escalator scare, we went to the movie theater in the same mall. We were sitting in the large hallway of the mall waiting for Susan to buy the movie tickets. I was off to the side near some large windows sitting alone. I watched people walk by. I must have forgotten my situation for a while with the excitement of the escalator. I got a quick reminder when a group of young people my age walked past me. They all got very quiet as they walked closer.

They looked right at me. I knew they were wondering what was wrong with me.

I turned the wheelchair around and I saw my reflection in the large window. I felt sick. I looked like a skeleton wrapped with skin. My right leg stuck straight out in front of me wrapped in a large bundle of gauze and ace wrap. I was wearing a back brace to keep my broken back from collapsing. It stuck out over the top of my t-shirt. Until that moment, I had always seen myself as I used to be, not as I had become.

> *September 12: Bret in chair. Saw himself in window and hated it. His denial caught up with him. Help us Lord!*

The next morning I was in the therapy room again. I saw someone I had not seen there before. He was an outpatient by the name of Siede. He was a young man in his early twenties from the Middle East. Siede was crumpled in a wheelchair that reclined backwards to fit his stiff and curled posture. He could not have weighed more than one hundred pounds. He had thick black hair and his head was rolled over to the side with a stream of drool hanging from the side of his mouth. There was a catheter bag of urine hanging on the side of his wheelchair.

I slowly wheeled past him and over to Julie. "What happened to him?" I whispered.

"That is Siede. He was here at the University of Minnesota studying to be an engineer. A truck hit him when he was riding his bike," she whispered back.

I felt terrible for him. A bright young student with promise for a good life suddenly struck down to nearly nothing.

"Will he ever get better?" I asked Julie.

"No. He has a severe brain injury. He has been like this for over a year. He comes here once a week for therapy just to keep his muscles loose," she explained.

I have never forgotten Siede.

* * *

I had been at Sister Kenny Institute for nearly three months, yet I had not gotten to stand up in the parallel bars once. It had been nearly six months since the accident. I was up in the wheelchair and getting very independent. It was as if I were living there as a tenant. Alan and I spent hours hanging around the nurses station late into the night harassing the night nurses and having fun. Every day we spent a good part of the day going to the cafeteria eating and laughing.

Since Alan and the other "quads" could not use their hands, I usually fed them. They were given braces for their hands and arms, but it was too clumsy to get much to eat.

"Hey, you stinking para," Alan complained, "Shove some of them there taters in my mouth, would ya?" Alan opened his mouth as wide as the halo on his head would allow.

Just the way he said it made us laugh so hard I could hardly handle the task. In most cases that would seem somewhat socially unacceptable to say such a thing. But there was hardly a person there who would tell us that. The people in the cafeteria must have thought we were from another planet. How could these guys in wheelchairs and seemingly enduring such tragedy have so much fun? It was simply our way of trying to accept what we were going through.

We were getting well known by the hospital staff and some of the more regular visitors. They usually saw us heading down the hallway with Alan hanging onto the back of my wheelchair while I pulled him along with mine.

We were on our way from the cafeteria back to our room. Just outside the cafeteria was an obstacle that challenged us each day as we left. It was a wheelchair ramp with a steep incline. Going into the cafeteria was fun because it was all downhill. But, coming out was uphill.

We refused to accept help from concerned passers-by. Instead, Alan and I wanted to do it ourselves. It was easy for me to go up the incline because I had full use of my arms. Although Alan was getting movement back in his arms, they were still very weak. He could hardly push his wheelchair on a flat surface, much less up an incline.

We tried to maneuver the ramp different ways. I tried to pull Alan up as he hung onto the back of my chair. But that didn't work because his fingers were not strong enough to hang on as we went up. Our only other option was for me to push him up.

I got behind him with my right leg sticking straight out, and I pushed on the backrest of his wheelchair. I gave him a big push and we traveled a foot or so. Alan quickly grabbed the wheels, holding himself from sliding backwards. I repositioned myself while he held on. Then I gave him another big push. After about five or six pushes, we were at the top, having won a small victory over our obstacle.

After we maneuvered the ramp, we changed positions. I got out in front of Alan and waited until he positioned his wheelchair behind mine. He reached out and hooked two fingers in between my back brace and my back. I pushed back on my wheelchair backrest to provide pressure on his fingers. That locked him into "pulling position." I took off, pushing my wheelchair and pulling Alan in his.

"Hey, man. You've got two good arms. Pull, man, pull!" Alan yelled as if he was riding on a dog sled and I was the dog. We streaked down the hallway. I leaned into each push, pumping my arms harder and harder, going faster and faster. Steering my wheelchair while pulling another proved difficult. We usually swerved back and forth down the hallway as if we were the only ones ever to use it.

As we picked up speed, my wheelchair began to veer off to the right. I noticed we were getting dangerously close to the wall. I did not realize Alan's wheelchair had been swerving back and forth and fishtailing behind mine as we sped along. Suddenly, I heard a crash behind me.

"Aaahhhh!" Alan yelled.

I looked back and saw Alan had let go. His wheelchair steered right into the wall. His wheelchair hit the wall, and he flew out of it slamming to the floor with a hard thud.

"No!" I cried, "Alan!"

He was on the floor unable to move. I spun my wheelchair around and raced back to him. He was out of the halo, but his neck was still healing. I was scared he broke his neck again.

"Alan!" I cried again.

I heard him groan and looked closer. There was blood coming from his forehead.

"Ooohhh! Don't tell me you broke your neck again!" I cried.

Finally, I heard his voice. "You got too damn close to the wall! Where'd you learn how to drive that thing?"

"Are you all right?" I demanded to know.

"Yeah, I'm fine. I just don't have the strength in my arms to get up off this stinking floor," he complained.

About that time our least favorite nurse came around the corner. "I thought I heard the two of you. Now look what you've done," she said, scolding me. She called for some other nurses and tended to the wound on Alan's head.

"You'll be all right. You're lucky you didn't break your neck again," she said with a sharp tone as they lifted him back up into his wheelchair.

"What? Can't a guy have a little fun in this joint?" Alan replied.

"A little fun?" she challenged, "You two will be lucky if you ever get out of here at this rate."

We went to our room after that and talked into the night again about getting out of the hospital. Together, we fantasized about living a normal life again. I continued to dream about the day I would walk again. Alan was walking pretty well by this time with crutches. I still believed I was going to walk again, but it could not come soon enough.

Finally, one day Dr. Day came to visit. After much begging, she finally agreed to let me try to stand up in the parallel bars.

"Bret, I just don't want you to be disappointed. You really do not have much movement or any strength to do this," she explained.

"Just let me try. I know I can do it!" I declared with confidence.

The next day in therapy, Julie led me over to the parallel bars. "Looks like today is the day," she announced with excitement in her voice. "Are you up for it?" she asked.

"Am I up for it? I've been waiting for months!" I replied.

Julie lined up my wheelchair to the end of the parallel bars and let down my right leg. She put a thick belt around my waist so she could hang onto me when I stood up.

"Okay, grab the bars and let's get you up," she said.

I grabbed the parallel bars and started to pull. The natural instinct kicked in and I pushed hard with my legs. I was surprised when the full weight of my body swung under me as my legs crumpled, yet I was still pushing up hard with my arms. My mind shifted to my legs alone and I concentrated on pushing with my legs, but they were limp and offered no help to stand.

My denial must have deceived me into thinking that standing again would be as easy as it was before the accident. People stand using their legs without thinking much about it. My legs did nothing. I quickly shifted my weight so I could push myself up using my arms only. Julie pulled hard on the belt around my waist, helping me to stand.

Finally I was standing! I felt the room spin. The last time I stood was before the accident. I hadn't even thought of what it would be like standing with paralyzed legs. I watched Alan do it and it looked easy. His legs lifted him up and he balanced himself with his hands on the parallel bars. But it was much different for me. I had no strength in my legs. They were no help lifting me up.

I stood in the parallel bars with most of my weight on my arms. The pain in my back turned to an intense burn. It felt like there was a fire burning inside of me. I could feel myself shaking.

"How long has it been?" I nearly whispered.

"Oh, about thirty seconds. Do you want to sit down already?" Julie asked cheerfully.

It seemed like I had been standing for hours, but I was in too much pain to feel embarrassed.

"Yeah, I better sit for a minute," I replied with a heavy sigh.

I lowered myself down with my arms. I never dreamed the wheelchair would be such a welcome place. As I sat regaining my composure, I began to feel ashamed. It felt so good to sit down; and after all that begging to stand up in the parallel bars, I did not want to try it again.

> *Sept. 27: Parallel bars. Tried too hard on his legs.*
> *Bret had hard night, so much pain.*

I wanted my life back, but I did not consider the cost. Freedom comes at a cost. The cost of freedom from that wheelchair was pain.

Chapter 9 – Going Home

The marching band played loudly and the cheering crowd rocked the small gym. The referee's whistle broke through the noise of the cheering fans, stopping the basketball game. Unfortunately we came in late and quickly became the center of attention as I rolled my wheelchair into the gym. I had just gotten home from Sister Kenny Rehabilitation Institute a few days earlier. The last thing I wanted to do was go to the basketball game that night. Instead, I wanted to hide from the world. I was embarrassed of the paralysis, my weakness. I did not want anyone to see me.

The gym was full of people who had been hearing rumors of my condition for the past six months. Now they were able to see first hand. People began to crowd around me.

"Hey, Bret, you look great!" Linda, a long time friend, said with excitement in her voice.

Behind me, a familiar voice broke through the noise, "We want you to know, dear, if there's anything you need just let us know." She put her hand on my shoulder. Looking around I saw it was Connie, another family friend and a big supporter of our town's athletic teams.

In the middle of all this, a group of young girls ran up to me. All at once they tried to hug me. Another group of small boys who I coached in little league baseball a few years earlier were pushing in from the side with little room to fit in, each asking different questions at the same time.

"Bret, can you walk yet?" little Charlie said as he grabbed my leg and pulled on it.

"Hey, can I have a ride?" another boy, Chad, said squeezing in.

It was like going home to a family reunion. I felt loved. But at the same time, my insides were ripping apart. My entire identity was caught up in being respected and admired for athletics. I was fighting my new identity: Paralyzed and too weak to walk.

The next morning Mom stopped by April's house to pick me up for my first physical therapy session at the hospital in Huron, South Dakota. April opened her home for me to stay until my parents' home was made wheelchair accessible. A makeshift wheelchair ramp had already been built so I could get in and out of her house.

Mom was fumbling around in the kitchen waiting for me. "Bret, where do you want me to put your pills?" Mom asked as she stood in April's kitchen.

She was holding a shoebox full of medication bottles. There were twelve different kinds of pills. I took most of them three to four times a day. I hated it. It seemed to me that one was supposed to take care of side effects from the other, which took care of side effects from yet another. Those pills were not in my plans.

"Just throw them away, Ma. I'm not taking them anymore," I said as I transferred from the bed to the wheelchair.

"What? You can't just quit taking them! You'll wind up right back in the hospital," Mom argued.

I countered quickly, yelling from the bedroom, "Well, I'm not taking them. I think those dumb pills are part of why I'm not getting any better. I should be walking by now!"

"I'll just leave them here in the bathroom and you'll have to take them," she answered giving up the argument quickly, not believing I was serious.

"Can you come over here and help me with this?" I asked.

"What do you need?" Mom replied.

"I'm taking this back brace off too," I continued, "It hurts. And, besides, if I'm gonna get stronger, I can't have this thing on all the time."

"What are you doing?" Mom protested.

"I've put up with their ideas of how to get better long enough!" I stated, "I'm doing things my own way from now on."

After that day I did not take any more pills, and I did not wear the back brace. Mom worried constantly about those things, but I had to do it my way. I felt that if I did not take charge of my own life, I would never get out of that wheelchair. Although mom worried, she had the wisdom and patience of a saint. She let me do things my way so I could discover what I needed for myself.

Mom helped me get into the car and put the wheelchair in the back seat. We drove away from the house and headed for Highway 34, a four-lane highway that runs through our small town of Woonsocket. I used to spend hours with my friends cruising up and down the "four-lane" growing up. Large trees along the side acted as a canopy and provided a sense of warmth as we drove. We drove past the home I grew up in. It is the kind of house one would expect to see in a small town. It was an older white two-story with a screened in front porch.

Main Street looked the same. My best friend in high school was Jeff Jenssen. His dad owned a grocery store that was a hub of activity for the small Main Street business community. Across the street was the bank, and across from that was the post office. Down one block further was our family business, Don's Silver Dollar Bar and Grill.

"Do you want to stop, Bret?" Mom asked.

"No. I just want to get up to Huron to see what therapy is going to be like," I replied, wanting to avoid reality by seeing people I knew.

The twenty-minute drive was interrupted only by the growing pain in my back from sitting upright too long in the car. Mom walked alongside me in the wheelchair as we entered the hospital.

The hallway was cold and sterile with a familiar smell. I figured all hospitals must smell alike. The rehabilitation department was in the basement.

The elevator doors opened to a long hallway. I liked pushing the wheelchair on tile floors. It rolled easily and moved fast. When in Sister Kenny, I learned how to quickly turn corners by reaching my hand out to touch the wall. The chair followed tightly around the corner. I also liked popping wheelies and spinning circles to make the ride less boring and giving me a sense of adventure. I decided to make the best of it by having some fun while sitting in it.

We made it to the rehab department. "Hi. I'm here for some rehab," I exclaimed.

"Oh, you must be the new guy from Sister Kenny," a nice-looking younger gal with sandy-blonde hair replied as she walked toward me. "My name is Bobbi."

I liked her already. "I sure hope you can do more than that other place," I said referring to Sister Kenny.

"What do you mean?" Bobbi asked innocently.

"All they would let me do is sit in this wheelchair. I went there to walk, not sit around," I complained. "Are you gonna help me walk?"

"Well what's stopping you?" Bobbi countered. "I don't see you doing anything but complaining. If you want to walk, you better get going."

I really liked her now!

Bobbi took me into a small room with a mat on the floor. She instructed me to get out of the chair and onto the mat. She did not offer any help. I was impressed.

"The first thing I want you to do is lie on your back and lift your legs up as high as you can," she instructed further.

I quickly got down onto the mat and lay on my back. I pulled with all my might to lift my legs, but the best I could do was drag my left knee up with my heel dragging on the mat. My right leg still could not move.

"Well, that's a start," Bobbi said.

"Hey, what's going on in here?" another nice-looking gal with blonde hair walked into the room. "Who's this?" she demanded.

"Hey, Mary, this is Bret. He's the new guy I told you about from Sister Kenny," Bobbi replied.

"Well, aren't you a cutie," Mary said.

I really liked this one. "Hi," I replied.

"So when are you going to get off that mat and walk for us?" Mary said.

"I'm working on it. It won't be long," I said as I accepted her challenge and struggled to lift my left leg.

"You better try a lot harder if you think you're ever gonna walk! Is that all the higher you can lift that leg?" Mary said with a sarcastic tone in her voice.

I loved Bobbi and Mary from the day I met them. They were not condescending, and they constantly challenged me. They talked with a positive attitude and a joyful tone in their voice. There was no "defeat" in their words or their tone.

I left physical therapy that day happy to find a place willing to work with me. I finally found some help. Everyone there, not just Bobbi and Mary, talked positively. They challenged me and even playfully teased as they worked with me to meet my goals. It seemed so different from Sister Kenny where they decided I would never walk again without even giving me much of a chance.

I learned a valuable lesson that first day in therapy. When people make up their mind about something, their actions usually follow in that direction. The people at Sister Kenny made up their mind that I would never walk again because of the statistics from medical research, together with all the people they see each year who never walk after a spinal cord injury. But now I found people who were willing to give me a chance.

> *"Therefore I tell you, whatever you ask for in prayer,*
> *believe that you have received it, and it will be yours."*
> *- Mark 11:22*

Mom and I drove home that night happy and excited. We both felt like our prayers were being answered. When we got home we were in for even more good news. Dad and several guys were taking measurements of the house. Dad usually did things without consulting Mom. The day he bought the bar and told the family we were moving from Rockford, Illinois, to South Dakota was the first day Mom even knew of the plan.

We pulled into the driveway at home and saw Dad working on the house with some other guys. "It's about time you got home," he declared from a ladder high on the side of the house.

"What are you doing up there, Don?" Mom inquired.

"Bret, where do you want the ramp?" he asked.

"What ramp? What are you talking about?" I yelled from the car still trying to get the wheelchair out of the back seat.

"We're building an addition onto the house so you can move home. The deck will go right here," he explained as he pointed down from the ladder.

"Hey great! But you better not spend too much money on the ramp, cuz I'm not gonna need it for long! Just put it over there on the south end," I yelled back excited to see the new construction activity.

That's the way Dad usually did things. He got an idea and went with it. The addition to the house started that day by tearing siding off the house and nailing boards in place. As night grew on, the work stopped and the work crew headed to the bar. They were the regulars at the bar. Dad was always a popular sort of guy. He had the kind of personality that drew people to him. Owning the bar was just the icing on the cake. They loved being his friend and helping him, but they loved that he owned the bar and they could drink for free when they helped him with a project. It was a good time of friendship and community.

Mom drove me to therapy for the first few days, but I decided it was not too cool to have my mom drive me everywhere. I needed to figure out a way to get around by myself. I have always been independent. From the time we moved to South Dakota I was pretty much on my own. Mom and Dad were always working at the bar. I rarely had to answer to anyone. Even back in Rockford I spent most of my time doing what I wanted to do. Mom and Dad both worked and I had the run of the neighborhood. I loved my freedom.

Realizing I needed to find a way to drive myself, I sat in Mom's car wondering how I could do it. It was a 1978 Ford Pinto. Jana was usually the one to come up with names for things. She somehow found a nickname for everyone and everything. She called this car "Pauly the Pinto." It was red with a stripe down the side.

I sat studying the controls. I was told we would have to put handicap controls on the car for me to drive. That was not an option, feeling like that would mean I was giving up, and I did not give it a second thought. I looked down at the gas pedal and the brake, studying them intently. After a long time staring at the inside of the car, I finally had a thought.

"Hey, Ma!" I yelled.

I looked up and whistled for her when I did not see her coming, but after a few minutes she faithfully came walking out of the house. It was the fall of 1986, six months after the accident. The weather was beautiful for that time of year with the temperature in the sixties.

I yelled, "Hey, Ma, run in and get me a broom, would ya?"

"What do you want that for?" she replied, questioning my intentions.

"Come on, Ma! Can you please just go get me a broom?" I pleaded.

Looking puzzled, she went to get me a broom. I felt the anticipation build as my plan came together. A few minutes later Mom came out carrying a broom. She walked up to the driver's side of the car where I was sitting.

Standing next to the car, but holding the broomstick safely out of my reach, she demanded, "Now, answer me. What do you need this for?"

"Just watch and learn," I answered playfully with confidence.

She reluctantly handed it to me. I started the car. I positioned the pointed end of the broomstick down under the dash. I bent over to look under the steering wheel to see where the end of the stick was hitting. I guided the broomstick down to the gas pedal and pushed it down. The engine revved.

Mom's eyes got really big and she cried, "What are you doing? Give me that back."

She reached in and tried to grab the broomstick. "Oh, no!" I said, stopping her from grabbing it. "Watch! It works great!" I said excitedly.

"You're gonna kill yourself. I should have kept you in the hospital!" she cried in playful frustration.

I looked down under the dash again and used the end of the stick to hit the brake pedal. After pushing it down a few times I moved the broomstick over to the gas pedal again. Then I switched it back and forth, practicing as if I were driving.

"See ya later, Ma!" I cried cheerfully as I grabbed the shifter on the floor between the front bucket seats and put the car in reverse. I hit the gas pedal with the broomstick and backed out of the driveway. Poor Mom stood there helplessly.

I waved goodbye, pressing the gas pedal down with the stick and drove away.

* * *

I was making real progress after six weeks of physical therapy with Bobbi and Mary. I spent every day, Monday through Friday from one o'clock to five o'clock in the afternoon with them. They worked with me on many different exercises. My favorite was standing in the parallel bars. My left leg had gotten strong enough to support my weight as I stood, but I still had to use my arms to hold me up. My right leg was not strong enough to do anything.

One day Bobbi had the idea that I might be able to walk if I used a brace on my right leg. She explained it would be the type that locked my knee into place so it would not buckle underneath me when I put weight on it. Within a few days I was fitted for a brace. It was a perfect fit for my skinny leg with no muscle.

It was an exciting day when I got the long-leg brace for my right leg. Bobbi also had a brace made for my left leg called an AFO brace. That brace locked my ankle in a ninety-degree position, because I could not lift my foot up. I still had no movement below my left knee. I sat in the parallel bars as Bobbi helped put the braces on my legs. My heart began to pound as I thought about what this meant. It was the end of November. Six long, life-changing months had gone by. I was excited. I hoped with all my heart this was the day I would walk.

Bobbi sat in front of me as I sat in my wheelchair. The braces were now on and fit perfectly. She pushed down on my right knee locking the long-leg brace. It clicked as it snapped into place. I could not move my knee even if I wanted to against the steel and leather of the brace.

"Well, are you ready to stand up?" Bobbi asked. She was standing in front of me between the parallel bars and Mary was next to me.

I slowly grabbed the parallel bars. Taking a deep breath I lifted myself up, locking my arms like a gymnast performing his routine. I let my weight down and felt my body press down as the weight shifted onto my legs. Pain burned deep into my legs and a tingling sensation flared intensely as I stood for the first time with all of my weight on my legs instead of my arms.

"Can you let go of the bars with your hands and try to balance?" Bobbi asked. "Watch it, though. You're not used to standing yet," she instructed.

"Hey, look, Merk, you're standing!" Mary said with a shout of joy.

I felt the chrome bars under my hands get slippery with sweat. I stood as straight as I could and quickly lifted my hands off the bars. Instantly my head and shoulders flew forward as if someone shoved me from behind. I quickly grabbed the bars tightly catching myself as I flew forward.

"Whoa!" I shouted, catching myself.

"I figured that would happen," Bobbi said. "You haven't used those muscles in your back for six months. They're not strong enough to hold you up. You jack-knifed forward." Instructing further she said, "Try throwing your shoulders back further to keep from falling forward and let go with your hands again."

I stood as straight as I could, shifting the weight of my head and shoulders back as far as I could. It felt awkward. I knew I would not be able to walk that way. I dismissed the thoughts going through my mind and tried to lift my hands off the bars again. This time I fell forward, but not as fast. I kept trying, throwing my head and shoulders back as far as I could and quickly lifting my hands off the bars.

Finally after several tries, I was able to stand. I balanced for about five seconds and had to grab the bars again. It was the first time I stood without using my arms since the accident, but I was too tired from the intense pain to feel happy about standing. I dropped down to the wheelchair wondering how I was ever going to walk again if it was so hard to simply stand.

Day after day we practiced standing. Soon I was able to balance for several minutes. Learning to take steps came next. Holding myself up with my arms made everything seem easier. I could take small steps forward in the parallel bars, but only when my arms held me up. The obvious problem I faced was that I could not take the parallel bars with me.

Bobbi had an idea. I was sitting in the wheelchair between the parallel bars, and Bobbi brought over a walker. It was the kind mostly used by older people to help them walk.

"Why not give this a try?" she said.

Suddenly my world got very bright. "What a great idea!" I thought. It would be like taking the parallel bars with me.

My mind raced with thoughts of leaving that place using the walker and throwing away the wheelchair. I quickly moved my wheelchair into position in front of the walker and locked the wheels in place. I grabbed the handles on the walker and looked up at Bobbi. She was standing in front of me.

I pressed up and shifted my weight forward, putting all my weight on my arms. Bobbi reached down and pushed my knee back, locking the long-leg brace into place. I stood straight with my head and shoulders back trying to let the weight off my arms. I tried to push the walker forward so I could take a step. The walker felt like it was glued to the floor. It would not move an inch. I leaned my head and shoulders back as far as I could and tried to push the walker forward again, but it did not work. I stood there trying for several minutes not wanting to give up. This was my big chance to walk, but it was not working. I could not move.

I sat back down and slumped into the wheelchair feeling like a failure. I was mad and sad at the same time.

"I'm not going to walk. They're right, I will never walk," I complained as I sat quietly feeling sorry for myself.

Bobbi looked at me and said, "You're just not ready. It's too soon. We'll keep working in the parallel bars. Don't give up, Bret."

Something in my countenance was different than Bobbi or Mary had ever seen before. The usual joyful confidence was gone, replaced with defeat. They were uncomfortable, I could tell. I just wanted to get out of there. I wanted to be alone.

I drove home. It was a dark November night. Tears rolled down my face as I thought for the first time the doctors were right all along. As I drove along the lonely highway towards home, I thought of how I was going to live the rest of my life paralyzed and weak. As my denial slowly washed away, I began to accept that my old life was over. My stomach hurt. I felt lonely.

I never considered that my condition would be permanent. From the earliest days after the accident, I believed I would walk again and get back to my old self. It seemed to be just a matter of time. But reality was hitting me hard. They were winning and I was starting to believe them. I was losing my hope again. I was losing my fight. I wanted to quit. The tears kept coming.

> *"You shall remember all the way which the LORD your God has led you in the wilderness these forty years, that He might humble you, testing you, to know what was in your heart, whether you would keep His commandments or not."*
>
> *- Deuteronomy 8:2*

Chapter 10 – Step of Faith

The prairie wind howled through the streets of our small town in the heart of South Dakota. The dark night produced an eerie feeling as I drove aimlessly for hours. Along the way I passed familiar sights triggering memories that worked their way into my heart. They were pushed aside by self-pity. Tears continued to stream down my face.

I talked to God, angry and hurt as I drove. "God!" I demanded, "I thought You were going to heal me. I thought You would let me walk again."

The agony built. Alone in my car I screamed, "I trusted You!"

There was no response. Only silence.

There was no room in my heart for God's plan. All I cared about was to walk again. Walking became my hope. The idea alone was my new god, my idol. Through all the surgeries and pain of the past several months, I fully expected God would heal me completely. But the tragedy continued and was getting worse. I was not being healed.

I finally went home to bed. It was dark. The same eerie feeling went with me from the streets to my room. I felt alone and scared. I lay in the dark wearing headphones and listening to a song from Michael W. Smith. The words of the song were about "darkness" and "evil" in the world around us. The words seemed to fit the darkness in my heart.

Thoughts ran wild through my mind. Woonsocket, built in the late 1800s, was not set up very well for people like me. My thoughts ran to a place far away where I could hide. I imagined life in a place like Minneapolis, Minnesota, where I could find handicapped housing and accessibility. When I was there at Sister Kenny, I saw many places where disabled people lived.

The deeper truth in my heart was that I could not face people who knew me before the injuries. I wanted to run away. I thought that if I had to live my life in a wheelchair, it would be easier if I did not have to face people who knew me before I got hurt. My desire to run away was just another form of denial, but it was the only comfort I could find.

I prayed again as I lay in bed, "God, where are You?"

"I will never leave you, nor will I ever forsake you."
- Hebrews 13:5

By this time I was no longer demanding, I was pleading. I wanted God to tell me everything was going to be okay, that it was all a bad dream. I wanted to wake up from my nightmare and be my old self again.

Suddenly, in the midst of the darkness, the room became very bright. I looked up at the ceiling for a light, but I knew in my heart the light was not of this world. It was brighter than anything I had ever seen, yet it was soft and warm.

Just as suddenly as I felt the light, something very strong and powerful from within me said, "Go to Snyder Drug and get forearm crutches."

"What are forearm crutches?" I thought to myself, "Snyder Drug?"

I was excited. The words fit the light. I could tell they were one and the same. I did not actually hear words. There was no voice, but the words were powerful and specific. I knew it was God.

He broke through my darkness when I had no more faith to believe. God spoke to me. I knew it was my Lord. My excitement grew. I had never heard of Snyder Drug. Peace filled my heart. I quickly drifted off to sleep.

"I am with you always."
- Matthew 28:20

The next morning I woke up excited like a small child on Christmas morning. My world was full of light. The darkness in my heart was chased away by a few simple words. I knew God spoke and I knew I was going to walk again.

I called Mom who was down at the bar. "Mom!" I almost yelled, "Have you ever heard of Snyder Drug?"

"Well, yes. There's a Snyder Drug in Huron. It's right on the main road as you go into town," she answered. "Why?"

"God told me last night to go to Snyder Drug and get forearm crutches," I exclaimed. "Come over and get me, we're going to Snyder Drug!"

A short time later, what seemed like hours, Mom stopped by April's house to pick me up, and we drove the twenty-mile drive north to Huron. We talked as we drove. I told her the whole story of the night before. I explained how I tried to walk with the walker, but it did not work. She listened quietly, not sure what to make of the whole thing.

My excitement grew as we entered town. I saw the sign: Snyder Drug. Mom steered into the parking lot and helped me get the wheelchair out of the car. She held the chair steady while I transferred over from the car into the chair using my arms. I grabbed my legs with my hands and pulled them up, putting them in place on the footrests of the chair. Each time I had to do that I felt sick to my stomach. I never got used to it.

Mom opened the door as I pushed the chair into the store. A bell hanging from the door jingled when Mom opened it. A lady stood behind the counter and looked up when we came in. She politely greeting us.

"Hi," I said. "Do you have any forearm crutches?" I asked as I wheeled closer to the counter where she was standing.

"Why, yes. These are forearm crutches," she replied as she reached over a few feet from where she was standing and grabbed them. It looked like a cane with a bar extending above the handle grip. At the top was a band that fit around the forearm to make the crutch more stable.

"Would you like them?" she asked with a smile.

"Yep, I'm gonna walk with them today," I announced proudly.

"Well, that's wonderful. I hope they work for you," she answered.

Mom paid for them and we headed over to therapy, only minutes away. She helped me out of the car again and carried the crutches as she followed me into the hospital. We went down the elevator one floor to the basement and wheeled down the long hallway towards the therapy room. My wheelchair glided effortlessly on the shiny, smooth tile floor as we moved along.

Bobbi was standing in the middle of the therapy room when we arrived. Mary was further back helping a patient on the leg extension weight machine. I wondered what she was going to think about the crutches. I popped a wheelie and spun around, quickly stopping the spin and popping the front wheels up even higher.

"Stop that!" Bobbi commanded. "You're going to fall back and break your head open, or give me a heart attack, one of the two!"

"Hey! See these forearm crutches?" I declared confidently, "We're gonna walk today!"

Bobbi looked down at me with a somewhat puzzled look on her face. She knew I left the day before upset about the walker. I could tell she was thinking the crutches were not going to be any different.

"Are you sure, Bret?" Bobbi tried to talk sense into me, "Maybe you just need more time in the parallel bars."

"Nope, I'm gonna walk today!" I announced again.

Bobbi looked over at Mary. "Well, are you coming?" she asked Mary.

I felt confident as I positioned the wheelchair down the long hallway. Bobbi asked Reid and another guy to help. They were both big men and able to hold me up if I fell. Bobbi wrapped a thick

Velcro belt around my waist. It had handles on each side for the therapist to hold me up. Reid and the other guy grabbed the handles. Bobbi gave me the forearm crutches and I slipped my hands through the top loops fitting them tightly around my forearms.

Standing directly in front of me, Bobbi said, "On the count of three."

There was a silent pause, "Ready! One, two . . ."

"Wait!" I said.

Only seconds earlier I was confident and excited, ready to walk for the first time. But fear quickly stopped me. I looked down the long hallway and then down at the crutches. I was afraid to fail again. I did not want to face it. I was suddenly hot. The sweat began pouring out. I slumped in the chair wanting to turn back, to hide.

> *"Faith is the assurance of things hoped for,*
> *the conviction of things not seen."*
> *- Hebrews 11:1*

Just then I remembered the rainbow when I was in the hospital, and the light that came to me in the dark room the night before. As my mind went back to those memories, I felt myself straighten, sitting up in the chair again. I could feel the confidence was coming back, but this time it was not my confidence. I felt it deep on the inside. It was an inner strength. It felt real, not pretend like usual. I knew I could do it. I took a deep breath.

"Okay. I'm ready." I declared.

"All right . . . One, two, three!" Bobbi counted.

They lifted me up. The belt dug into my waist and I felt it pull me up. I pushed with all my might on the handles of the forearm crutches. I leaned my weight on them trying to get my balance.

"I've got ya. You won't fall" Reid said firmly as he and the other guy balanced me.

I felt pain burn in my legs and back. I pushed the pain aside in my mind looking down the long hallway. It looked much longer than it did before. My knees were locked and my hands gripped the crutches tight. I was terrified again but determined to face it.

Bobbi explained what to do next. "Put all your weight on both legs and on the left crutch. Then, lift the right crutch and move it forward a little bit."

I tried to lift the right crutch, but it was cemented to the floor. I leaned to the left, shifting my weight so I could lift the right crutch to move it, but I felt like I was going to fall over. Reid moved in closer on my left, putting his hand on my shoulder to steady me.

"You're okay. Just keep going," Reid instructed.

I held my breath and clenched my teeth. Leaning back hard, overcompensating for the sensation of falling forward, I quickly lifted the right crutch moving it forward about six inches. I dropped all my weight back onto both crutches again and felt safer.

"Now put all your weight on both crutches and your right leg. Then move the left leg through," Bobbi said.

I was scared. I felt like I was standing on top of a tall building and she just told me to step off of it.

> *"I can do all things through Christ,*
> *who gives me strength."*
> *- Philippians 4:13*

I looked down intently at the shiny tile floor directly in front of me and took another deep breath, putting all my weight on the two crutches and my right leg. I lifted my left leg from the hip and swung it through. It moved forward about three inches. I locked my knee hard as I put weight back onto it.

"Good job!" Bobbi congratulated me with excitement in her voice. "Now put all your weight on both legs again and shift your weight onto the right crutch so you can move the left crutch forward."

My back was burning and I was already sweating. I had just taken my first real step since being paralyzed. I could not quit. I gritted my teeth and kept my eyes on the floor directly ahead of

126

me. I did not want to risk losing my concentration by looking up. I did just as Bobbi told me, putting all my weight on both legs and the right crutch. I shifted my weight to the right and quickly moved the left crutch forward and put it down again. I was ready to take my next step.

This step would be harder than the first because of the long-leg brace on the right leg. I could not bend at the knee to move it. I had to lift harder from the hip to move it forward. I leaned to the left and lifted hard with my right hip. I felt my right leg move forward. It moved a few inches.

I did not know how much more I could do, but I had to keep going. It seemed like I had been standing up for hours, but it was only minutes. This was harder than any workout I had ever gone through for sports. Repeating Bobbi's earlier instructions, I took another small step.

I could hear murmuring from people standing in the hallway and watching. Excitement was building in the basement of the hospital as word traveled fast of the paralyzed kid taking his first steps. People slowly began to emerge from the kitchen and other rooms. Cooks, janitors, doctors and nurses were slowly filling the hallways to watch.

Each step was like a marathon. I paused to regroup after each one. Step three, four, five, six. I needed to sit down. My hands were slipping on the handles of the forearm crutches from sweat. I paused wanting to stop.

"You can do more, Bret. Great job! You've taken six steps. Let's see if you can do more," Bobbi challenged.

Seven, eight, nine, ten, eleven . . .

After twenty minutes of fighting to walk for the first time, my back was on fire. It felt like a hot iron was placed on my lower back. My arms were shaking, sweat was pouring out of me.

"Do you need to sit?" Bobbi asked.

"Yeah," I replied quietly, too exhausted even to speak.

Mary quickly placed a chair behind me. Applause erupted as I sat down. Those who gathered cheered and congratulated me. I was on top of the world! I was even thankful for the burning pain in my back. Twelve steps! I walked twelve awesome and glorious steps that day. I started my own journal and wrote,

> *Nov 19: Today I walked 12 steps with the forearm crutches for the first time! Please don't let the progress stop now! Thanks for being with me this far!!*

> **"But in all these things we overwhelmingly conquer through Him who loved us."**
> *- Romans 8:37*

I left therapy flying high. I was so excited as I drove south towards home thinking about the day and the night before. I felt so strong, so loved. He answered my cry.

> *"He will call upon Me, and I will answer him;*
> *I will be with him in trouble; I will rescue him"*
> *- Psalm 91:15*

* * *

Almost as quickly as it all came together, it began to fall apart again. I was on an emotional roller coaster ride, which seemed to me to be a nightmare straight from hell.

> *Nov 21: Well, back to reality. . . . . I did the same as yesterday in therapy but it seemed 100 times harder! God. . . You have to give me the ability and strength to do this. There's no way I can do it on my own!*

Each day at therapy was a high or low on the roller coaster ride. I could not see past the day. My eyes were fixed on my progress and my heart demanded perfection. I could not see walking the rest of my life with crutches or a limp. Although I was not even able to walk more than a few steps, I was already worried about *how* I was going to walk. I wanted what I wanted, and I wanted it now.

> *"The testing of your faith produces patience."*
> *- James 1:3*

My hope was grounded in my progress at therapy. I hoped to walk normally again more than I hoped to be like Christ. My hope being in the wrong place led me to turn to those things that many do to ease their pain. I went out with some friends to drink away my problems. Coming home from the hospital presented new challenges. When I was fighting to live, there were little temptations to do wrong. But now that I was working my way back into normal living, the temptations were lurking about to destroy me further. The spiritual battle was raging around me. It was a pivotal point in my life. The forces of good and evil were fighting for my attention.

> *Nov 23: At first I thought it was a hangover but it turned out to be the flu. Whichever it actually was, drinking has to end. I'm gonna have to concentrate more on getting back to myself. From now on I want to live for God and getting back to what I use to be (physically)! God. . . allow me to build this feeble body back to what it was, and better! And then allow me to give the glory to You! Please make life better for me!*

An older couple, the Wilsons, invited me over to their house. Although I had never met them, I knew they were believers and often traveled to Sioux Falls, South Dakota, (one hundred miles southeast) to attend church. I was not sure what to think about their invitation, but I figured there had to be something special about them since they traveled so far to go to church.

I drove over to the Wilsons' and pulled the wheelchair out of the back seat. I transferred over to the chair and wheeled towards the house.

"Hello, Bret," Mrs. Wilson said as she came out a side door of her house to greet me. Wearing a dress and an apron, she looked to be in her sixties with gray hair.

"Hi, it's nice to see you," I replied.

I was thankful to see their house had no steps to get in the front door. The only way I could get up stairs would be to get out of the wheelchair, sit on my rear-end and push myself up each step with my arms. That would have been humiliating to me. It was amazing how such small things were huge obstacles being confined to a wheelchair.

"Come on in," she invited pleasantly, "I've made some cookies for you."

Mr. Wilson walked out of the living room as I wheeled into their kitchen. He was tall and looked to be in his sixties as well. I recognized both of them from around town. The house was a small one story with wood floors. I liked that because the wheelchair was easy to maneuver, unlike on carpet.

"Bret, I'm happy you're here." Mr. Wilson was business-like and got right to the point. Mrs. Wilson did not even have time to bring in the cookies. "God has been telling me to call you over for prayer," he said with unusual boldness.

"Sure, that sounds great," I quickly replied with an uneasy feeling in my stomach.

I was surprised. This was the first time we had met, yet he talked to me like we had known each other for years. I looked straight at him and wondered if this was going to be "the day."

"Will this be it?" I thought to myself, "Will I be healed today?"

Mr. and Mrs. Wilson walked over to me. Each placed their hands on me, and Mr. Wilson began to pray. His prayer was loud. He sounded confident. I listened quietly, waiting with my eyes closed tight. I could feel his warm hands on my shoulders as he prayed louder and louder.

Suddenly, nearly shouting by this time, he prayed, "In the name of Jesus, I command you to stand up and walk!"

Obeying his command I pushed with all my might, trying to use my legs without any help from my arms. I struggled, pushing harder with my legs. Realizing nothing was happening, I shifted my weight forward and pushed even harder placing my hands on my knees. I pushed harder with my hands.

Nothing. I did not raise up one inch from the chair. I sat in silence looking down at the floor wondering what was happening.

"Now, Bret. I don't want you to be upset that you didn't stand up and walk today. This kind of thing happens. We just need to do some work with you," he explained.

I listened quietly.

He continued, "Your faith is not strong enough right now for you to be healed."

"No!" I thought in my head, "That's not right."

He continued to explain why his healing session failed due to *my* lack of faith. "We need to teach you how to speak in tongues and grow your faith so you can be healed." I wondered why he thought it was my lack of faith and not his own. Finally, I had heard enough.

Looking at him I replied quietly, "Mr. Wilson, God told me that He is healing me, and that I will walk again. But He is building my character in the process so it is taking longer." I was not sure where those words came from. They just came out. I never had those thoughts before that day.

"No!" he yelled directly into my face. "God does not want you to be like this. This is the devil's doing!"

I was stunned. My heart filled with anger. I could not believe he said that to me! I wondered how anyone could say such a thing, especially to someone in my position. I began to see how people can shut off the light of Christ in them by their own ambition.

However, I did not understand it at that time. I was confused and hurt. I just wanted to get away from him.

> *Nov 24: I'm feeling especially down and defeated today. God . . . please make Satan leave me alone! Can't I experience victory and triumph continually? Haven't I been through enough?*

> **"Let us continually offer the sacrifice of praise to God."**
> *- Hebrews 13:15*

It was odd, but it seemed the deeper the pit and the darker the valley, the clearer I could hear God's voice. I knew God had spoken to me about my healing, but it was hard to remember as I struggled to fit what He was telling me into what I wanted. I was being tossed around again like a ship on the ocean during a huge storm. If I made some measurable progress in therapy, I was on top of the world. But if not, I was down as far as I could get.

At the same time, my friends tried to get me back into doing normal things, but I resisted. My ego was getting in the way. I fought to keep my pride. I did not want to face people paralyzed and weak, unable to walk. Little did I know that was one of the deeper issues God was working in me to change, my ego.

> *Nov 25: I went to therapy today and it went pretty good so I was in a great mood. Dana asked me to go watch the college basketball game so I did. Boy did that hurt! I hated it! It made me see how different I am. I'm ashamed to be this way!! When people see me, whether I know them or not, I want them to be impressed and maybe even in awe at my physical being! But now all they do is look at me with pity. God, please let me be what I used to be. Lord, allow me to be something I don't have to be ashamed of!!*

> **"When He has tried me, I shall come forth as gold."**
> *- Job 23:10*

Each day in therapy was a measuring stick. In my mind, the measuring stick was my progress in walking. But God had a different measure. God's measure was that of my faith. I had no choice but to rely on Him, to trust Him. But I fell. Most days I was not trusting in Him at all.

> *Nov 26: Therapy went pretty good again. I walked pretty far. From the rehab doorway to the end of the hall. There is so much that goes with walking that no one really thinks of. I feel like I'm in prison! Sure I can go most places, but I don't want to this way! I'm ashamed of it! Please God, let me out of this! I can't do it but You can! I don't want anything half way. Please Lord, let me walk and run!*

"The glory of a young man is his strength."
- Proverbs 20:29

I was sliding down a slippery slope, headed for a hard landing. My focus was inward, on myself. There was nowhere to run. I could not manipulate or talk myself out of this situation. Doctors could not help me. My family could not help me. My friends could not help me. I was unwilling to work this out with God. It did not seem to matter what I learned before or how good I felt after God helped me in the past. I wanted it my way or no way. It was a constant fight within myself.

> *Nov 28: Therapy went ok. I hate this, though. Nothing is worth this! Out of all things, why paralysis? Especially me. Right now I don't feel like there is a God. I know I've come a long way since the accident, but this isn't near enough! I can't help but think of SAM all the time!! Sure I may walk, but like before? I know SAM will consume me! I can't go on like this. I can handle the scars, but not this paralysis!*

SAM was my code word for suicide.

Chapter 11 - Confusion

It was early December, nearly seven months after the accident. I had been home from the hospital for several weeks by this time. Each night I slept for at least twelve hours because my body was working hard to recover. I would normally wake up from a long night's sleep and watch the Andy Griffith Show. After that I ate lunch and went off to therapy for the day.

Every day was the same. Get up, watch a little television, go to therapy for the afternoon, and back home to the high school gym for more walking. My progress at therapy for that given day would dictate my emotions until the next day at therapy.

> *Dec 1: Therapy was awesome today! I worked hard and walked well. I walked with one hand in the parallel bars today, so that means a cane is not far away. I'm really excited about my progress, but it scares me that I might get too excited for nothing! Can this be true? God will not forsake me! He wouldn't bring me this far and drop me!*

God was digging the foundations of my life deep into my heart. At no other time did I learn such basic truths about myself, life, and God.

Each day was a new struggle with the emotions of how these injuries were affecting me.

> *Dec 2: Well, here we are. Another day goes by and I'm still in search of what this is all about. Will I ever be happy? Why doesn't God help me out? I feel as if He doesn't even want me or care about me.*

135

Will I ever have a joyful, happy, fulfilling spiritual life? This life isn't worth diddly! When I was growing up I was so blessed physically, and now I have nothing!!

Before the accident I had been trained through the world, the media, and my peers that I deserved to be happy in this life. Back then I believed if there was a God, He existed to make me happy. Yet God was breaking through those crumbling stones that made up the foundation of my life, and He was replacing it with solid-rock foundational stones of new beliefs and new values through the things He was showing me.

Dec 7: God, I feel like I've been robbed! This just isn't fair!! I don't want to be this way. I don't deserve this. I don't want to go through life ashamed and embarrassed of myself. God, give me what I used to have. Allow me to hold my head high and be proud!

**"Do not work for food that spoils,
but for food that endures to eternal life."**
- John 6:27

For a young man in his early twenties, few things matter more than how he looks to others (especially girls) and how much fun he can have. I was one of the worst of them. In those days my idea of a good and happy life was getting what I wanted.

Friends were constantly streaming into my parents' home to visit. I wanted to make sure they were there for the real me, not the memory of me. Being popular and a successful athlete in a small town is like being a celebrity of sorts. It becomes even more interesting after being paralyzed in a terrible accident, the curiosity and drama of it all takes over.

It hit me hard one day when I got into a friendly wrestling match with Dana, a good friend three years younger than me, while we were watching television. I was lying on the bed with

Dana next to me. Jeff Jenssen was my best friend from high school. We affectionately called him "Dub," which was short for Double J. He was sitting in my wheelchair trying to pop a wheelie without falling over backwards.

It got started when Dana stole my pillow from under my head. I waited until he placed it comfortably under his head before jerking it out and causing his head to fall hitting the steel bars of the headboard. He grabbed my arm and squeezed it in retaliation. Knowing I was useless from the waist down, I quickly grabbed a bar at the headboard of the bed with my left hand for leverage. I twisted the other arm out of his grip and quickly grabbed his arm, squeezing even tighter than he did, meeting his challenge.

Before I knew it, he swung his legs up and twisted around, landing on top of me in a split second. He hooked one arm around my leg and his other arm around my head. I was suddenly locked up tightly in his powerful grip. I tried to straighten my body, pushing hard with my leg, but there was no strength to get away. I was helpless without my legs.

"Get off me you jerk!" I yelled, "or I'll sick Dub on you!"

I acted like it was all fun and no big deal, but I was embarrassed and hurt. I knew he meant no harm, but I wished I had my legs back for just a minute.

Although my life was turned upside-down, I tried hard to hide my feelings. All the people constantly stopping by made it seem like a never-ending party. All my visitors were amazed at my great attitude, which was just a cover-up most of the time. I wanted to give up and quit nearly every day, but I had to keep up the show.

> *Dec 14: People don't look at me as "Merk" any-more. I hate the way they look at me now! But for some reason I know God is going to restore me! Whenever I get bummed or depressed, I feel God very strong inside of me telling me not to panic; be patient. Okay. I will and the Lord will deliver me. I know it! Thank You, Lord. I praise You!*

My entire motivation and focus was on getting back into the physical shape I used to be and learning how to walk perfectly. After working hard at practicing how to walk at therapy for several hours in the afternoon, I came home each night and went down to the high school gym to lift weights and practice walking more.

Dub was going to college in Mitchell, South Dakota, about thirty miles away. He faithfully drove home every night to help me walk in the gym.

"Are you ready, Merk?" Dub asked as he stood in front of me waiting to start our next lap around the gym.

"Yeah, let's get rolling; I'll beat you this time," I said with a challenging tone in my voice. I pushed hard on the forearm crutches as Dub lifted at the belt around my waist and steadied me as I stood up. I took a deep breathing knowing it would take me a long time to walk around the gym floor. Not wanting to put it off any longer, I took my first step as we began our journey.

Dec 17: I am going to the high school gym at nights now. I'm up to one lap around the gym floor. I want to build up to a lot of laps without stopping.

I was sweating heavily as I took the last few steps back to my wheelchair, completing another lap around the gym. Dub, walking sideways and holding onto the belt, continued to encourage me to work hard and shake off the pain.

"Merk, it doesn't get any better than this! How many people can say they were completely paralyzed and learned to walk again?" Dub remarked as he encouraged me to finish the lap strong.

"Not many, I suppose," I replied with a shaky voice. "I just wish I didn't have to be one of them," I replied with a tone of sarcasm. "Why couldn't I be finishing strong in my last lap of a quarter mile race?"

"You were never that good at running anyway," Dub replied with a teasing tone.

"Watch it, pal, or I'll take you down and teach you a lesson," I challenged. "Don't forget to respect your elders, young man." Dub was two years younger.

Dub was a state champion half-miler in high school one year before my accident. I was there at the finish line to congratulate him. We used to run and train together. We were both quarter-backs on our high school football team and worked out during the summer throwing the football and improving our skills. When we were not working out, lifting weights to get ready for the next sports season, we were racing our motorcycles around town and chasing girls. A few years later, I was working to improve an entirely new set of skills to win an entirely different sort of race.

> *Dec 18: The pain is not getting better. When I walk it hurts so bad I want to die! My right foot hurts from the time I get up till the time I go to bed!! God . . . allow me to win!*

God gave me small encouragements to help me along the way. One such encouragement came when I went to see my doctors for a check-up. Mom and I made the hour-and-a-half trip to Sioux Falls. Dr. Benson, a nice-looking man in his fifties with his hair beginning to gray, walked into the room.

"Bret, you're doing amazingly well after all you've been through," Dr. Benson stated as he began to examine me.

"Well, I sure appreciate all you've done for me, Dr Benson," I replied.

"Let's see if you can wiggle these toes," Dr. Benson instructed.

"I still can't move them. I can lift this leg up, though," I said as I grabbed my left leg.

"Well, let's see it," he replied.

Still sitting in my wheelchair, I lifted my left leg straight out in front of me and locked my knee.

"Wow, that's great!" Dr. Benson exclaimed. "How about the other one?"

The right leg was still in the long-leg brace. Although I could lock it when I would take a step in the leg brace, I could not lift it up from a sitting position. Still in the wheelchair, I lifted my right leg and pulled it forward to an extended position. I let it go and the ankle dropped down to the floor.

"You still can't lift that leg up, huh?" Dr. Benson questioned.

"No. The best I can do is lock it out when I'm taking a step. The brace helps," I replied.

Dec 21: Went to Sioux Falls today. Dr. Witzkie said I was a medical miracle and Dr. Benson said I was the closest he ever saw to death and come back. He also said I should write a book.

"He who began a good work in you, will perfect it until the day of Christ Jesus."
- Philippians 1:6

Jan 2, 1987: Marie came to see me. We had a great time!

* * *

The storm continued to rage, letting up for small periods of time but then hitting harder and coming back with a vengeance. January of 1987 was a long, hard month where God did some of His greatest work in my life. I was learning to trust Him the only way we can, by having no other choice.

Jan 8: I feel like God has given me an inner confidence that everything will be okay. Just work hard and everything will be fine! I have to train harder than as if I were training for the Olympics!!

Jan 10: How much more can I take? Am I fooling myself or will this get better? Walking hurts so much! Will I ever get rid of that wheelchair? I never realized how fortunate I was before the accident! Life sucks! I think this is about it! I don't want to live if it has to be like this! I think about SAM all the time.

Jan 12: I don't know what's worse, the pain or trying to hide the pain. I don't ever want to be a complainer. I want to endure this with my head held high and a smile on my face.

Jan 15: Life & Happiness: I can't go through life expecting so much. I just need to find joy and happiness in whatever it is I find myself doing. I'm just going to be happy wherever I am with whatever I'm doing.

Jan 18: I want to be normal! I guess I just can't worry about a thing. Take life day by day and enjoy each and every one of those days—and trust in God. I get into trouble when I start worrying about the future. But it's my nature to worry, then I get ticked off at God. I know He understands—I just hope things work out with God and me.

Jan 20: When I get the most depressed is when I look at what I have become compared to what I expected to be. Then I about die! Out of all the possible ways life could have turned out, I obviously went down the worst possible path. I can't believe this is actually happening to me. For some reason I just thought God loved me more than this. But even as I write this, I feel this overwhelming light of hope inside me. I feel so strongly that life is going to get incredibly better for me!

Jan 26: I'm getting very impatient! I'm sick of being like this! When will I get out of this wheelchair? If I'm not on a flat surface, I can't walk. So that means the only place I can walk is in the gym or the hospital! God, please get me out of this wheelchair!

Jan 27: Why me? What did I ever do to deserve this? This isn't fair! How can God expect me to praise Him and be thankful in this situation? This is no way to live and go through life. But I do anyway because I don't want to be disobedient to God. Maybe because of that obedience God will bless me!

Jan 28: Today in therapy I walked from the therapy room to the elevators and back. I had to work so hard and it hurt! And it's so slow. That's not walking! I can't handle this!! How can God do this to me?

Jan 29: I don't know if I can take any more! No way am I going to live like this! God doesn't care about me!

Jan 30: I'm pretty down lately. I've never felt so humbled and helpless (out of control). What's so wrong with wanting to be normal and do the things I used to do? That's not too much to ask! And when that happens, I'll remember this time and be filled with joy because of my second chance.

Feb 1: Will I ever get over this depression? I'm thinking, what's the use? I have to quit thinking about the old me—he's gone! But I can't accept this!

It was a dark night in early February of 1987. Dub and I just completed another lap around the gym. Sweating and tired I sat in my wheelchair with Dub guiding me to my seat. I threw the forearm crutches on the floor in disgust.

I complained bitterly, "This is so hard. It's never going to be worth anything. It takes so long to walk anywhere. I think the doctors are right, I'll never be able to walk normal."

"Merk, you just got rid of the long-leg brace! That's progress," he countered.

"Yeah, but look how far that set me back. It takes me twice as long to walk. I feel like I am going to fall every time I step on that leg." I was inconsolable.

I looked up at the clock on the wall next to the large basketball scoreboard. It was nine o'clock in the evening. I slumped in my chair. Looking up at Dub I bitterly complained, "That just took an hour! One hour to walk around that gym floor just one time!"

Dub had no response. After a long silence, anger replaced the depression in my heart. I said, "Come on; let's go."

I sank into the car seat. "Let's go get some beer," I said defiantly. We drove to dad's bar and talked the bartender into giving us some beer. After drinking for a while, Dub dropped me off at home. It was another dark, eerie, winter night as I struggled up the ramp and into the house.

I was feeling lower than at any other time in my life. After two months of working harder than ever, I suddenly gave in to the doubts. I knew deep inside things would never be the same as before. I was going to have to live my life this way. Nothing I could do would ever change that.

I felt completely empty. I lost my legs, and I lost the hope of faith in a God that would heal them. I could not understand why He would tell me "No" in my prayer for healing. I thought God existed to answer my prayers. But there was no fighting Him. It was His way or no way. I longed to escape this nightmare, but there was nowhere to go. I could not run from God and His divine answers in my life. I hated that I could not get my way. I could not accept this defeat. But I had no choice.

143

It was late in the evening. I sat alone in the dark dining room facing Mom's rolltop desk. In the top right-side drawer was my answer. It gave me new hope. I sat staring at the drawer, falling deeper and deeper into a trance-like state. It seemed like I was in a different world where no one else could enter. I felt numb.

I reached out to pull the drawer open. I hoped it was still there. I saw it just the day before. Over the past month, I had gotten into the habit of checking each day to make sure it was there. Both excitement and fear grew as I pulled open the drawer. There it was. I picked it up and held it in my hand for the first time. It was heavier than I thought it would be. The wooden handle seemed to fit my hand perfectly. I slowly spun the bullet chamber to make sure all six were loaded. They were.

Without hesitation, I lifted the gun to my head and pointed it at my right temple. I felt the cold silver barrel push against my skin. The gun made a clicking noise as I pulled back the hammer. With my finger resting on the trigger, my mind began to race. I felt for the first time in a long time that I was back in control of my destiny. This was it. A showdown between me and God, my will against His.

Anger filled my heart as I sat with the gun pointed to my head. "God! How can You do this to me?" I angrily screamed in my mind, "I won't live like this! You can't make me live this way!"

It seemed my whole life came to this climactic point. Everything I lived and hoped for came down to this moment in time. If I could not have a life that pleased me, I would have no life at all. I sensed evil swirling around me, urging me on to win this fight. I felt the pressure of the trigger on my finger as I sat in angry defiance of God, as if taking my life were some type of retaliation.

I closed my eyes, waiting. Nothing happened. No noise, no pain. Just silence. I still felt the pressure of the trigger on my finger.

The gun did not go off. Something made me put it down. The fight was over.

"He caused the storm to be still,
so that the waves of the sea were hushed."
- Psalm 107:29

I sat with shoulders slumped, head low, eyes closed, and defeated. It seemed like hours before I could move, not knowing where to go or what to do next. I finally turned the wheelchair around and headed back to my room. I gave the wheelchair one last hard push as it glided towards the bed. The chair hit the mattress and the momentum catapulted me upward, throwing me face down on the bed.

Breathing heavily into the sheets, I prayed softly, "Lord, what do I do? I can't live this way. Please, God, please!" I begged.

The anger was gone, replaced by sorrow and self-pity. Finally the tears came and then I began to sob. Hardness was turning to brokenness as I lay sobbing, my will shattered to pieces.

Sobbing into the sheets, I drifted off to sleep.

It was not the physical fight that wore me out. It was my fight against God's will. My hope was to walk normal again and to live without pain, but my hope was in the wrong place. That night as I slept, God transformed my heart. He was showing me how to hope in Him alone, and nothing else.

"The sacrifices of God are a broken spirit; a broken
and a contrite heart, O God, You will not despise."
- Psalm 51:17

Chapter 12 - Victory

The day seemed like most others in therapy. I showed up at the usual time, around one o'clock in the afternoon. We practiced walking, riding the stationary bike, and working out my feeble leg muscles. Bobbi and I were in the parallel bars again. It was a small room with the parallel bars running nearly the entire length of it. Medical equipment cluttered the corners of the room.

Dropping back down into the wheelchair, I sat taking a break while talking with Bobbi and Mary. "I wish I could take those parallel bars with me wherever I go," I sighed. "It feels pretty good walking in there," referring to the stability of the bars which made me feel safe from falling. Falling was a constant worry. Not only could I get hurt worse, which would set me back further, but I could not get off the ground if I was by myself when I fell.

Bobbi replied, "They give you the stability your muscles are lacking." She was always teaching me about my condition.

Mary jumped in. "Oh, Merk, just hang onto the arms of all those girls; that'll give you stability," she remarked in her usual teasing tone.

"Girls?" I contended, "What girls?"

"Come on, we know what you're up to after you leave here every day!" she teased.

"I wish! I just go home and work hard like a good little boy," I teased back.

As we talked, I noticed a walker standing alone over by the wall. I looked at it for a moment while Bobbi and Mary talked. Their voices blended together as I got lost in my thoughts. I was thinking about the last time I tried to use it, how I failed and drove home that night feeling like God failed me. But things were different this time. I was not afraid. Much had changed since I tried to use the walker last. I felt confident I could walk with it this time.

"Hey, do you think I should try that again?" I asked as I pointed to the walker, quickly turning the conversation to a more serious tone.

"Well . . ." Studying the walker Bobbi replied, "I don't see why not."

Mary could not resist, saying, "Yeah, give it a try. The girls will love it!"

Bobbi brought the walker over and placed it in front of me. It had been three months since I tried to walk with it. I quickly grabbed the handles. I pushed with confidence and determination, using my arms to lift myself up and out of the wheelchair. I quickly stood to my feet. It felt much different than the first time. I steadied myself. Arching my back to gain balance, I pushed the walker forward, leaning on it as I took a step: First with the right leg, then with the left.

I was surprised I could do it. I glided through each step, using my arms and the walker to do much of the work. The difference this time was due to all the work in the parallel bars balancing and strengthening my low back muscles. I did not realize I had improved. It allowed me to take enough weight off the walker to push it forward. Then I shifted my weight back onto it when I stepped through.

Heading out the door and looking back I said with satisfaction, "Come on, we're walking outta here!"

Bobbi followed in the wheelchair. She rolled slowly next to me as I walked. It was the same hallway where I practiced walking, in the basement of the hospital near the therapy department. The floor was covered with a light colored tan tile, and a soft grey painted block made up the walls. The hallways were long and turned directions twice before reaching the elevator several hundred feet away. As we passed the kitchen, I heard pots clanging and people talking.

Step, slide, step, slide, step, slide. The walker made a sliding noise as I pushed it forward in front of me to take my next step. Each time I stepped, I leaned forward with my hands tightly gripping the walker handles, putting most of the weight on my arms. It was a very slow process. We talked about the past and the future. That helped me keep my mind off the pain. After several steps I stopped to rest, stretching my back by arching backwards. Then I began again, step, slide, step, slide, step, slide.

Although Bobbi knew my condition well, I had not told her much of what I experienced in the hospital before I came to her in the therapy department. This was a special time we shared. I explained how the doctors did not give me or my family much hope, and the staff at Sister Kenny Institute advised me to accept the reality of life in a wheelchair. I took each step with determination as we talked. It was like trying to talk while exerting extreme effort. My words were halting and I paused frequently. Bobbi responded softly, mostly listening and giving words of encouragement.

We walked together the entire distance out of the hospital all the way to my car. It took close to an hour, but it seemed like only minutes. Bobbi helped me put the wheelchair in the backseat along with the walker and I drove home. My feelings of elation were overwhelming. Nine long months had passed since the day of the accident, months of hoping to walk again and to be normal, and months of that hope being shot down continually by doubt and fear. But this was a new beginning born of a hope coming true. I walked to walk, not to practice walking. That walk out of the hospital took me somewhere. It was useful.

When I arrived home, Mom's car was parked in the driveway. It was dark. I sat in the car staring at the back deck on the house trying to decide what to do next. A wheelchair ramp ran along the back of the deck with railings on each side spanning the distance. I had to grab the railings to pull myself forward in the wheelchair when going up the ramp, otherwise I would tip backwards because the ramp was so steep. I would pull hard to propel myself forward a few feet and then quickly move my hands further up the rails grabbing them again, catching myself before I rolled backwards down the steep ramp. But going down the ramp was all worth the extra effort to get myself up it. I simply popped a wheelie and rode down.

I decided to use the wheelchair to get up onto the deck and carry the walker in my lap. It was tough pulling myself up the ramp with the walker in my lap, but I was excited to carry out my plan. I made it up the ramp and onto the deck, then rolled over to the door of the house. I lifted the walker off my lap and placed it in front of me. Pushing with my arms, I lifted myself straight up. It felt so good, so free to do that without someone standing next to me holding onto the Velcro belt usually around my waist. This time there was no belt, no assistance, just me standing alone at the door.

I arched my back trying to balance and quickly lifted my right hand off the walker handle to knock on the door. Knock, knock, knock. I waited. I did it again. Knock, knock, knock. Mom came through the kitchen and into the hallway towards the door. She squinted her eyes trying to see who it was. Opening the door, Mom looked up and saw me standing there.

Her mouth dropped and she stepped back nearly falling backwards. "Bret!" she exclaimed, "What are you doing?"

"Hey, Ma!" I proudly announced nodding my head towards the wheelchair, "I need you to take that thing and throw it down the steps into the basement. I don't ever want to see it again!"

> *Feb 10: I walked in and out of therapy for the first time and walked to the house for the first time! Bag the chair! Will it be for good?*

Only days after my fight with God, I escaped the wheelchair for good. I had no idea the answer was right in front of me each

150

day at therapy. He patiently waited for me to submit my will to His, and only then He let His plan move forward. How many times I must have wallowed in the misery of my self-centeredness when God sat by patiently waiting for me to follow Him.

Feb 11: I know God is with me, helping me and answering my prayers. I wore my graduation hat to therapy today - I told them it's cuz I'm graduating from the chair! I walked out of therapy and to the car. I'm using the walker but I'm out of the chair!! It's gonna be hard, but it's the transition.

Feb 12: It's been three days since I've used the wheelchair. It's great! But it's so hard - I don't want to go anywhere cuz it's such a chore!

Feb 19: I can stay miserable or God can perform a miracle and change my life. I read the book "Twice Pardoned" and felt excitement that the Lord will use me too. (Do something to make me feel special for Him.) It's giving me hope in Jesus. But I still feel pride and other things holding me back. These dark walls have been stopping me. I can't knock them down, God has to.

Feb 21: Never again can I say, "This is no way to live and go through life." From this time forward, I'm living my life for Jesus! Wherever and whatever the Lord has in store for me, I will rejoice!

Feb 22: I'm realizing this affliction and healing is definitely from God!! He's testing me – teaching me. He wants me to depend solely on Him!

Feb 23: People are their own worst enemies. Nothing is that bad unless you think it is! If you set your

*goals high, but be happy with what you have, you
should be fine.*

* * *

I continued to work hard every day learning to walk again and
staying close to Jesus. Walking was difficult because many of the
muscles in my legs did not work. They were still paralyzed. I was
able to use only a few of the many muscles needed to walk. Bobbi
estimated I had fifteen percent of normal muscle function in my
legs to work with. The muscles below my knees did not work at all.
On top of that, I felt it was important to walk straight and to look
as normal as possible when I stepped forward. It was very slow and
difficult.

I set a goal to go back to college in the fall of 1987 using just
one cane. That seemed impossible. To meet that goal, I stayed focused on one thing: Walking. I did not allow myself any extra pleasures. During this time, I only went to therapy and back home. I
did not want to give in to the desire to use the wheelchair because
it was easier. I decided if I could not go where I wanted by walking,
I would not go. Oftentimes I wanted to go with my friends out
to a movie, or to a restaurant, but it either took too long to get in
or there were steps or curbs that I could not get up or down. I was
determined not to let the obstacles get in my way or discourage me,
so I simply avoided them until I was ready.

This new attitude and focus came through my renewed commitment to God. My whole outlook changed when I stopped thinking
about my problems and started to focus on Him. I read the Bible
daily, prayed, and listened to music that glorified the name of Jesus.
When I did that, I felt renewed each day and full of life.

I woke up one morning to a beautiful spring day. I decided to
go for a walk down the block from our home. It was a new adventure. Thus far, other than walking to the car, I only walked in the
hospital therapy department and in the high school gym. I could

not walk very well outdoors because the terrain was uneven. I had to watch the ground closely when I took a step. If my foot stepped onto a crack, rock, stick, or some sort of bump, my knee buckled and I fell.

I enjoyed the walk outdoors on the paved road. I loved the feeling of walking to get somewhere. By the time I made it down to the end of the block, I was sweating and wanted to sit down in the worst way. Something I did not consider when I left the house was that there was no place for me to sit when I got to the end of the block. When I left I was alone. I liked the idea of walking alone down the street on my adventure. I enjoyed the rare feeling of independence. But I forgot that I needed someone with me if I fell. I had no choice but to continue back to the house. I finally made it home, exhausted.

God continued to give me more and more truth about Himself and what this life is really all about.

March 4: If I chose a life with the Lord, I can handle this. If not, the desires of the world will consume me!

March 23: So far since I've been a Christian, bad things have happened to me. But I know that God is working them out for the good. The Lord is such a part of me now. But when do the blessings and abundant life start?

March 27: I pray that I always remain humble in front of the Lord. I would like my life to represent Jesus. I would like to glorify the Lord. There's power in Jesus alone and His word. I pray I always remember that human nature has a tendency to take our eyes off Jesus.

I was getting stronger each day. I went from using the forearm crutches to the walker because it gave me stability. I felt safe. I could not stop using the wheelchair while using the forearm crutches because I needed someone to lift me up from a sitting position. My legs and back were not strong enough to stand up with the crutches. Since the walker had four legs, I could lift myself up with my arms to a standing position without having to balance as with the two crutches.

After throwing away the wheelchair and using the walker full time to get around, I began to get stronger and more confident. I used the walker for a few months and then began to feel challenged to make another transition. I began to wonder if I could start using the forearm crutches again, but this time I would have to figure out how to balance getting up and down. It was Saturday morning, a beautiful spring day, when my sister April came into my room. She made it a habit to stop over to check on me after I moved out of her house into Mom and Dad's. I was sitting in a chair next to my bed.

"Hey! How goes the battle?" she said with a cheerful tone.

"Oh, just staring at those forearm crutches over there, wondering if this is the day," I replied.

"Well, what's the holdup?" she quipped.

"It's not that easy, ya know," I argued in a playful tone, "I'm pretty comfortable with the walker."

"Yeah, but it can't hurt to try," she countered. April was quite the athlete growing up. She was confident and capable. We could have been twins we were so much alike. Jana was soft spoken like Mom.

"You're right, I just need to get on with it," I answered. "Hand me those things, would ya?"

I stood up using the walker and reached out as she handed me the forearm crutches. Slipping my hands through the forearm supports, I grabbed the handles and placed the crutches in front of me.

"Okay, can you move the walker out of my way?" I asked. She moved it out of the way and I stood leaning on the crutches.

"How's it feel?" she asked.

"Actually, pretty good!" I said.

Instead of leaning on them with all my weight like before, I was only using them to balance this time. My back and legs had gotten much stronger by walking with the walker to go places instead of using the wheelchair.

"Hey, I like this!" I cheered.

"Well, let's see ya walk with 'em," she challenged.

Bracing myself I took a step. It was not as stable as the walker, but it felt more like my legs were doing the work instead of my arms. I was surprised it was working so well.

"Looking pretty good," she said.

"Yeah, but now comes the big test. Can I sit and stand using these things?" I wondered out loud as I turned towards the bed to give it a try. Sitting down was not too difficult. Gravity did most of the work. But standing up was the big test. I tried several times to lift myself up, but each time I fell backwards onto the bed.

"Well, that's not working!" I said, challenging myself to press on. "Let's try something else. Can you hold this?" I asked, handing her one of the crutches.

I placed one crutch in front of me, pushing myself up with one crutch and bracing myself on the bed with the other free hand. Once standing, I leaned on the single crutch, balancing with it and pushed myself up the rest of the way. I stood balancing with one crutch.

"Okay, now hand it to me," I said reaching out for the other crutch.

This was a new phase, something I could not have done a month earlier. My back and legs were not nearly strong enough then. April helped me practice getting up and down, learning new ways to stand without having the strength in my legs to lift me up. I was gaining independence.

April 2: I went to crutches today. It's a step back
to go two steps up! I'm psyched! The Lord has really

been working in my life - both physically and spiritually. It' seems the more glory I give to God the better I get!

April 3: When I started with the walker it was so hard. But in the time I used it (2 mos) I got pretty good with it. Now that I'm using the crutches, it's pretty hard again. But in a few months I'll have 'em down pretty good. Hopefully I'll even get rid of one crutch!

April 5: I'm walking with the crutches. I feel like I can fall at any time. It's like walking on a tight rope all the time.

April 10: Am I going to have to go back to the walker? Please God - No! My back is killing me!

April 18: Hell is living without Jesus
       the frustration of life.
   Heaven is living with and for Jesus
       totally trusting
       relying on His word
       always yielding to Jesus.
   The harmony of God's plan
       the more yielding
          the sweeter it is.
   The ultimate goal
   Heaven itself
       no problems, no pain, no worries
   Just paradise!

Chapter 13 - True Love

July 2: All I want is to be a whole person again!

I was inching my way towards the goal of walking with just one cane. I could barely walk with two forearm crutches, let alone just one cane. Yet after a few months of fighting hard everyday to walk with the forearm crutches, I challenged myself to move on to using two canes. It was another step back to take many more forward. I hated those transitions. Just when I got comfortable enough to walk to places other than therapy and the house, I made a transition and could go nowhere else again. But there was no other way.

It was late July 1987. Dana and I drove three hours south and east of my home to Vermillion. We were there to register for the fall semester classes at the University of South Dakota. Getting on with my life was exciting, yet scary. Dad previously urged me to continue with school. I told him I was thinking about skipping school for the fall semester.

He replied, "Well, where are you gonna live?"

"Live?" I said, "I'm gonna live right here with you and Ma."

"Oh, no you're not," he warned, "When school starts, you're either there or moving out and getting a job." Dad was wise in many ways. He helped me make many good decisions.

I walked into Slagle Hall to register for classes using two canes. It was a beautiful building made of heavy stone nearly one hundred years old. By this time I was becoming increasingly confident walking with the two canes. I still could not stand up or sit down without using the canes, but at least I no longer needed someone to help.

I was anxious because Marie Pletka worked at the Registrar's office. Marie and I dated on and off before the accident. I was excited and nervous to see her again. During the summer as the school year drew closer, I found myself thinking about her more and more. I walked down the long, wide hallway to the Registrar's office and came to a large window with a countertop running the length of it. Through the window was a large room with several desks and office equipment scattered here and there. I smiled when I saw her. She was standing at a table several yards from the window looking down at some papers.

"You gonna sign me up or what?" I asked teasingly.

She looked up showing her beautiful smile. My heart skipped a beat. I was stunned. Her beauty was breathtaking. Her deep brown eyes were captivating. Just over five feet tall and weighing not an ounce over one hundred pounds, she instantly stole my heart.

"Hey, you made it!" she said, "You look great!" We talked several times by phone over the past year and I called to let her know I was coming.

We decided to meet for lunch at a fast food restaurant. We sat in a booth and ate, talking and catching up. While we talked I kept noticing something different about her from what I remembered before. I could not quite tell what it was, but I liked it very much. I could have sat there all day talking with her.

Dana and I left for home. School was to start in a month. I did not think of much else but Marie until I went back.

July 24: Today we went down to Vermillion. It was terrible at first, but I remembered I prayed about it and I had to stay strong. Well. . . it went great! Saw Marie, she's so cool! I'm positive I'm going back to school! Thank You, Jesus! It's going to be tough – emotionally, but the Lord will get me through it. It's going to be the first step at being normal!

* * *

Dub decided to transfer to USD. We moved into Cherry Lane apartments for the school year and set up our apartment. It was obvious two male college students lived there. The living room was filled with a full Olympic weight set. Each day we lifted weights in our living room so I would not have to go over to the sports complex on campus to work out.

I was sitting in my room thinking of Marie. I hoped to see her now that school was starting. I was nervous though, because I struggled with thoughts of how girls would see me. I feared no girl would ever want me the way I was. But Marie did not seem to notice my problems. She looked at me the same as before, not seeing the horrible injuries and weakness.

It was a beautiful evening in late August 1987. The activities were electric as the new school year was getting underway. I heard a soft knock at the door. Wondering who it was, I yelled, "Come in!"

It was Marie. I could not have been happier. I was sitting on the couch, an ugly blue color that fit perfectly in our college apartment. Marie came in and sat beside me.

"How's it goin'?" she asked with her usual smile.

"Just hangin' out. Want to lift some weights?" I teased.

"Yeah, that'd be great! Let's hit them weights," she teased back.

"Looking like that?" I played along, "You better go change into your workout clothes." She was dressed for a night out on the town with her friends. I continued, "Where ya going?"

"Oh, we're just gonna see what's going on," she replied and asked, "Want to come along?"

"Oh, thanks, but I've got to finish lifting," I said, referring to finishing my workout.

I did not want to let college social life get in the way of my recovery. I wanted to be with her, but I didn't dare make it seem too obvious.

"Hey, what do you think about going out Saturday night?" I asked. "We could go to the Marina." The Marina was a nice restaurant in Sioux City, Iowa, thirty miles southeast of Vermillion. We went there together for our first date two years earlier.

"Yeah! That would be great!" she replied with excitement.

"I'll pick you up at six," I said.

"Sounds great!" she said standing up from the couch. "Well, gotta run. Mary and Lynn are waiting in the car." Smiling, she turned to leave. She hesitated, looking back as if she wanted to say more. I looked at her, nearly breathless, hoping she could stay.

"Bye," I said as she continued out the door. I watched out the window as she left the apartment building thinking Saturday night could not come soon enough. My heart soared as she left.

* * *

I fought my feelings for Marie. I was afraid to lose focus and wind up using the wheelchair because it was easier, faster. There were so many obstacles threatening my goals, threats like pain, inconvenience, my desire to get on with life again, and even my feelings for Marie. They all challenged my recovery. But nothing could be more threatening than the emotional pain that was to come. Back home I was surrounded by people who supported me. College was a different story.

I woke up the first day of classes at five o'clock in the morning. My stomach was sick with worry.

"Will I fall?" I feared. "I'm going to look stupid." My mind wrestled with thoughts, "Should I use two canes?"

Falling was my greatest fear. I was still obsessed with hiding the obvious. As a twenty-two-year-old college student, falling in front of my peers was the ultimate embarrassment no matter what I had been through. It did not seem to matter that I was still nearly completely paralyzed. I still could not accept it. To me it was plain weakness, which I hated. I did not think anyone could understand.

I read the Bible and prayed for strength before leaving. It was

160

my senior year as a business major. My first class was Business Policy at nine o'clock that morning. Praying as I drove to the business school, I circled the parking lot looking for the closest spot to the door. That became a constant habit. Fortunately, I found one in the front row.

Pushing on the car door with one hand and the seat with the other, I lifted myself to a standing position. I leaned on the car measuring the distance to the entrance. It was about thirty feet.

"Lord," I prayed, "please be with me. Don't let me fall."

Using the front of the car for support to step up the curb, I pushed off and began my journey. People were walking quickly by on all sides. I feared someone would run into me, knocking me over. A two year old or a strong wind could have easily done it. I kept my eyes focused on the ground directly in front of me, glancing up only to see how much farther I had to go. Each step I took began and ended with the cane striking the ground, providing only a small sense of safety.

I argued with myself as I stepped closer to the door, "Why not just use the other cane?" My thoughts blended in with the noise of people rushing by and my cane tip clicking against the sidewalk with each step. "But I can't! I'll never walk normal if I give in now."

I began to breathe once I got within a few steps of the door, knowing that if I fell I could fall towards the door to help myself back up. Falling further away meant I would have to crawl the rest of the way. I made it safely and wanted to rest on the door for a few minutes. I scanned inside the entryway for a safe path to walk. But I was in the way. Busy college students ranging in ages from eighteen to sixty were hustling to and from classes. Someone held the door waiting for me. He smiled awkwardly as I slowly made it through the doorway. I hugged the wall, forced by the flow of people into the large center hallway leading to the classrooms.

I practiced this journey the day before, so I knew where my first classroom was located. It was quite different the day before without all the people. I walked down the hallway, one hand gripping the cane and the other hand sliding along the wall for support. I began to feel more confident by the safety of the wall. That is when I noticed people watching me. I felt embarrassed as I realized what was happening. This was a different world. I did not fit in.

Thoughts swirled in my mind about this new world. In this place there were no special accommodations or considerations. There was no parade for making it back to school alive and back on two feet. There were no congratulations. It was just the cold, hard reality of getting back into the paces of life. Worse yet, my walking was worse than having a limp. I had to lean on walls and a cane. It was very slow, drawing much attention. I got in everyone's way. But I could not quit. I had to stay focused. I had to keep going.

Sept 1: Well, I'm at school now. I can walk for a while, but I get tired easy, then I can't walk worth a crap. I'm gonna keep my eyes straight ahead, work hard, stay in the Word!!

* * *

Marie and I were leaving class together a few weeks into the school year. It was raining, which made the tile floors extremely slippery. I put considerable weight on the cane when I stepped forward, which could cause the cane to fly out from under me when the rubber tip hit a wet spot. I scanned the floor constantly looking for water. I leaned on the wall carefully to avoid falling. People were walking around us. Once outside, I tried to be cool as Marie and I walked towards the car, acting like there was no problem. I did not want her to know I was afraid to fall. I did not even want her to know that it was a possibility.

Just then I stepped on an uneven crack in the sidewalk causing my right knee to buckle. I dropped hard onto the rain-covered sidewalk and pain shot through my hip and back. I was instantly angry, having realized my worst fears. Sprawled on the ground, people tried to help me up, making it seem worse.

Usually when people trip while walking, they look around to see what made them stumble. The embarrassment of the moment causes them to look for something to blame it on. Our minds naturally seek an excuse for our weakness. I had none. I was powerless to jump up and act like I simply tripped over a crack in the sidewalk. All I could do was sit on the wet sidewalk in humiliation.

Falling down seemed to me a cruel consequence of my injuries. The physical pain was nothing compared to the humiliation I felt. It was the ultimate proof of my weakness. God was slowly and faithfully transforming me into His likeness whether I liked it or not. He was showing me a new way. Instead of looking to myself for the answers and for a way to cover my weakness, I was forced to rely on Him to get me through.

> *"For those whom He foreknew, He also predestined*
> *to become conformed to the image of His Son."*
> *-Romans 8:29*

Falling is a submission of sorts. It made me bow. It was symbolic of my need to bow before God and His plan for my life. He was making me more like Him. It was so painful, yet He gave me just enough strength to get by. The strength He gave me that day was Marie. Her response to my fall was amazing. I could tell she was not embarrassed for herself or for me. It was as if Marie did not even notice. She picked up my book bag like nothing happened, and stood quietly waiting for me to get up. I knew she was special, but I had no idea of the gift that stood before me.

> *Sept 10: What a humiliating experience! Falling*
> *down in front of people walking to class. (It rained*
> *all day) Walking with a cane – noticeably a dork!*
> *God help me! It's okay though – God has brought*
> *me this far. It's a miracle and it's only the begin-*
> *ning!!*

"The Father of mercies and God of all comfort,
who comforts us in all our affliction."
- 1 Corinthians 1:3

I was beginning to discover the difference in Marie from before when we dated. We were together at the business school library studying. It was dark. Cars slowly passed by the large windows of the library. We were alone and talking about the accident. She began to tell me how she heard the news.

Her sister Julie left a note on the desk in her dorm room. The note read, "Bret's been in a serious motorcycle accident. Call me." Marie called and Julie relayed the news about the accident.

She continued softly, "They said you weren't supposed to make it. I couldn't believe it."

Marie's world took a turn that would change her life forever. She grew up quiet and shy. Her mother took care of all her problems, and she loved that feeling of safety. Marie's two sisters were there for her too. Having a twin who was very much like her but more outgoing made it easy for Marie to hide in her shadow. She liked it there, or wherever she felt safe.

Growing up for Marie was simple and carefree in her small hometown in southeastern South Dakota. Whenever there was trouble, her family made her feel safe. But she told me that no one could help her when she heard I was paralyzed and faced death. For the first time in her life, no one could help.

Marie continued, "Later, I went back home to the church where I grew up. I felt so helpless. I remember praying to God, 'Please don't let Bret die.'"

It seemed like Marie and I were the only people on the earth as I listened to her. I realized God was not just working on me through this.

* * *

The following months, through the semester and Christmas break, Marie and I saw more of each other. I still did not want to admit my feelings for her. I continued to act like we were "just friends," and that a full recovery was my main concern. But life was slowly getting back to something other than rehabilitation and recovery in spite of my ideas. Our relationship was becoming more serious. I anguished over it. She was God's gift to me in many ways. But I was blinded by my goals for recovery and did not see it until one night when we were together. It was February, nearly two years after the accident. Almost a year before to the day, I had taken my first steps with the walker and thrown away the wheelchair.

We were sitting on the couch in my apartment studying. It was getting towards the end of the evening and time for her to go. As she put her books into her book bag, she looked at me. Smiling, she pulled it onto her lap. Looking down, she began to zip it.

"I wish you could stay," I said, wanting fewer things more, but I knew she had to leave. It was getting late. She scooted over close to me. I reached out to hug her goodbye. We held each other. I did not want to let go. I could smell her perfume and feel her breathing close to me. Hesitating, she pulled back looking me in the eyes. I wondered if there was something wrong. Her deep brown eyes captivated my heart. She quietly began to speak.

"Bret, I've been wanting to tell you something," she said. My heart sank, fearing she was going to end our relationship. In the back of my mind, fear of rejection because of my disabilities was a big reason I fought my feelings for her. I perceived myself as only half a man. I could not believe that any girl could love someone in my condition. Rejection among everything else would have been too much. Yet I foolishly let myself get into this. I braced myself. I could not breathe.

She continued softly, "Bret?" Pausing, she looked deep into my eyes. "Is it okay if I tell you that I love you?" she said quietly, looking away as if she were preparing for her own rejection.

My heart leaped at the sound of her words. I could not fight my feelings any longer. She just opened the door of my heart. I could not keep it closed any longer.

I hugged her tightly and whispered in her ear, "Yes, Marie, you can say that. I've wanted to tell you the same for so long now, but I was afraid. I love you too."

We continued to hug for what seemed like a lifetime. Our hearts were knit together that night. It seemed like life was finally worth living.

> *Jan 14, 1988: I'm doing quite well. I guess I thought I would be farther physically, but where that lacks, God has allowed me to make up for it spiritually. Since I've come to school the time has flown by! I now concern myself with Marie and the thought of law school. I need to be strong and remain in Him. God will fix the rest.*

Chapter 14 - Blessing

Marie and I were married after my first year of law school. She worked hard to help put me through school and I finally graduated. We moved to Sioux Falls, South Dakota, where I took a job in a small law office. Marie and I were overjoyed when our first baby, Angela, came. She was the first of five such miracles. Each time we were blessed with a child, I recalled the doctors telling me I would never have children. After being blessed with five, Angela, Sarah, Ellie, Hannah and Joshua, I have learned that nothing is impossible with God. He gave me much to replace all I had lost.

Marie and I were having fun raising our children, and I continued to work at improving how I walked. It was important to me to look professional and walk well in the courtroom where I practiced law as a young trial attorney. But the pain continued to interrupt my ability to concentrate. I could not sit comfortably for even five minutes. The pain in my leg and foot often became overwhelming. It was all I could do to sit quietly without screaming in pain, let alone pay attention to the case. I did not want to let anyone know, even Marie, that I could not continue my career. I did anything I could think of to make it through my days.

I went back to my orthopedic surgeon several times for reconstructive surgery on my leg. He tried to make adjustments. After ten years of trying, I was back in the doctor's office looking for answers.

"Bret, we've tried everything," Dr. Cass said as he looked at me. I could tell he wanted to say something more. It was something in his eyes. "There's really only one more option." I felt it in my gut.

167

I knew what he was going to say. I dreaded this day, fearing it was inevitable.

Dr. Cass continued, "I think it's time to seriously consider amputation," he said holding my leg in his hands examining it further. It was odd to hear those words because they had never been spoken in my presence. Not since the hospital ten years ago was it ever discussed.

"I knew you were going to say that," I replied. "You've done everything you could. I think you're right." I could hardly believe the words I just spoke.

It was late in the afternoon in November 1995. Darkness was setting over the South Dakota prairie as I drove home. I called both Marie and Mom on the way. I cried as I told them what Dr. Cass said. I fought to keep my leg for ten years and still hoped for a full recovery, but amputation meant that would not happen. I would never be normal again.

"Father, if You are willing, remove this cup from Me;
yet not My will, but Yours be done."
- Luke 22:42

It took many years before I could even say the words paralysis or amputation. They were the worst things that could ever happen. Yet it was God's plan and I had to accept it. I had hung onto the verses in the Bible that promise healing, only to realize even that has to be within God's design and purpose. God's job was to execute His plan, and mine was to accept it.

I was in a pre-op room waiting for the doctor. It was a small, cold room with no windows. I was lying on the surgical cart with a heavy blanket over me. People were on all sides performing their various tasks in preparation for the surgery. A guy with a clipboard was at my feet looking them over.

"Now, which one are they removing today?" he said in a serious professional tone.

"Which one?" I yelped. He smiled realizing his game was successful in scaring me. Not one to back down from a challenge, I began to play along.

"Okay smarty, we're not taking any chances!" I instructed, "Get yourself a big black permanent marker and write 'WRONG LEG' on the left leg. We don't want any mistakes!"

The nurse at my head prepared an IV bag. Laughing at our banter she remarked, "Hey, that's not such a bad idea." One thing led to another and by the time they were done preparing me, the message to the doctor was written on my left leg in big bold black ink.

Soon after, they took me out of the pre-op room and headed for surgery. Marie and Mom were waiting in the hallway when they wheeled me through on the surgical cart. Marie was holding Sarah, our two-year-old baby girl, and Mom was holding Angela, our little four-year-old daughter. Angela, not able to understand what was happening to her Daddy, began to cry as they wheeled me past. She worried that she would never see her Daddy again.

The amputation went well. I woke up with a large cast on my right leg that ended just below the knee. I stared at the cast. It was odd not seeing a foot at the end of my leg. I argued in my mind, "It was so painful. It never worked right anyway!" The muscle graft made my foot like a club. A large flap of meat covered the top and the outside of my ankle. Walking with it was like walking with a sledge hammer at the end of my leg instead of a foot. It was heavy, ugly and painful. I was excited to get my "new leg."

After sleeping through the first day, I woke up ready to leave. The nurses told me amputee patients stay for at least three days, sometimes longer. But I had to get out of there, my little girls and Marie needed me. I talked Dr. Cass into letting me go early. We "negotiated" a deal: If I agreed to stay until lunch and if the nurses found my vital signs to be okay, then I could go.

Dr. Cass said I would probably have phantom pains, which are pains felt because the brain continues to communicate through the nerves after they have been cut off. The phantom pains were worse than any other pain I had ever experienced. It felt like the flesh on my toes and foot was being scraped off with a knife. There were intense tingling sensations and sharp pains like a knife stabbing into my foot. The worst pain felt like a large drill driving into the bottom of my foot. It drove through the skin deep into the flesh, continuing for ten seconds and then stopping for ten seconds. This went on every ten seconds, on and off, on and off.

At a follow-up appointment I asked Dr. Cass how long the phantom pains would last. He said they should go away after thirty days. Then he said something that haunted me, "In five percent of all amputees, phantom pains never go away." It was well after thirty days, and I worried that I was going to be one of the five percent. I forgot about all the times God took care of me before this. I lost trust in His plan again. The past ten years learning to trust Christ did not seem to help.

I arrived home from the hospital on a freezing winter day in January, 1996. I was on crutches, which I had gotten used to by this time. Over the years through the different corrective surgeries, I had to use crutches, the kind that fit under the arms. This time was different because I only had one leg to balance with. I also had no strength in the left leg to help, other than to stand. It was like walking on crutches and a peg. It was another transition like before. But this time I had a family and a job. I could not shut out everything else to focus only on my recovery.

The phantom pains were wearing on me and fought relentlessly to keep me down. It was well past thirty days from the amputation and I figured they should have stopped by that time. I began to wonder if I was losing my mind. Everywhere I went, the phantom pains went with me. One night I was sitting on the couch watching ESPN sports on TV. The phantom pains were not going away and even seemed to be getting worse. I was getting more and more angry about it. The stabbing pains were sharp. I could not take one more drilling sensation. Each time the pain hit, I prayed it would be the last. Then it would hit again. And again. And again.

After many days of trying to have a good attitude and apply all that I had learned in the past ten years through my tests and trials, I was at the same place I had been before. I wanted to give up. I was angry. Again, I was powerless to control the pain or my weakness. I was holding the TV remote in my hand when I finally blew. I reared my arm back and whipped the remote across the room.

I yelled, "I can't take this anymore!" The remote slammed against the wall, smashing into pieces.

Marie was sitting in a chair across the room. When she heard my cry, she jumped up and ran over to me.

Holding me in her arms she said in an unusually loud and confident tone, "Bret! The doubt you have right now, I don't have. The faith you don't have, I have. You will get better. The pain will stop. They will go away. Trust Jesus!"

I slumped into her arms, sobbing. I wanted to quit again. I just wanted to live a normal life. I was tired of being tormented.

* * *

I wanted nothing more than to be healed. At first I demanded it. But through the years I came to embrace the pain, seeing it as a blessing. It took me many years of hardship to learn that true victory is not winning the game. Instead, it is overcoming impossible odds when everyone says I can't, but God says I can. He did not allow me to walk perfectly after my injuries, but He did allow me to walk with joy. There is nothing in this universe other than God that can take away the strength in a young man's legs and replace it with joy in his heart.

Our struggles can either be a curse from the devil or a blessing from God. The devil's job is to kill, steal, and destroy. God's job is to give life.

> *"The thief comes only to steal and kill and destroy; I came that they may have life, and have it abundantly."*
> *- John 10:10*

He does that through the process of pain. In that process, God eliminates "self" from the equation. His miraculous transformation removed myself as the "focus" of my thoughts, plans and hopes, and it took me to a place where my Lord Jesus became the true focus and desire of my heart.

Our greatest revelations of God's love can come through our struggle against His will. It is a process where God shows us deep truth that we cannot find anywhere else or through anybody else. It has to come directly from Him. Normally, we are too busy to even think about such things. But pain slows us down, forcing us to take a "fast from the world" long enough to hear His voice.

In that struggle, we often ask the question, "Why me?" At some point we can get to where we are comfortable not having all the answers. God can transform our hearts to say, "Why not me?" or "Because God chose me." When "self" was finally out of the way, I was able to realize He chooses to use us in His mighty army to defeat evil and darkness, to change lives and to glorify Himself.

> *"For to you it has been granted for Christ's sake,*
> *not only to believe in Him, but also to suffer*
> *for His sake."*
> *- Philippians 1:29*

It is a great honor to be chosen by the Father for a special purpose. I had little hope until I discovered that purpose and believed He was in control.

Oswald Chambers wrote in his book, *The Place of Help*,
"There are times when the Heavenly Father will look as if He were an unjust judge. But remember that Jesus says that He is not. In the meantime, there is a cloud on the friendship of the heart, and even love itself has to wait often in pain and tears for the blessing of fuller communion. The time is coming when we shall see perfectly clearly, but it is

only through confusion that we can get to a clear
outline . . ."

Victory is finding the purpose for which we are called even
amidst the confusion and pain. It is to willingly walk in that plan.
The greatest victory of all time was when Christ endured the pain
of the cross for God to complete His work. His followers may have
to endure much as well and realize this life is about God's purposes,
not ours.

Although not all of us have to go through terrible tragedies in
order for God to use us, we all go through circumstances we don't
like. How we respond to those circumstances can make all of the
difference. Our attitude and our praise in the pain can bring about
victory. The blessing in it is overcoming tragedy and continuing on
with hope. It is praising God when we don't want to when it hurts
the most. It is overcoming "self."

> *"Let us continually offer up a sacrifice of praise to*
> *God, that is, the fruit of lips that give thanks*
> *to His name."*
> *- Hebrews 13:15*

* * *

After years of recovery, rehabilitation, and learning how to live
life as a walking paraplegic, God called Marie and I to start a ministry to help others by telling how God helped us through tragedy.

I called my sister Jana to tell her about our new adventure. Un-
surprised, she replied, "I wondered when you were going to start."

"Start?" I asked, wondering why she seemed to already know
about our plans.

"Don't you remember what you told me?" she asked. I didn't
know what she was talking about. She continued, "When I first saw
you in the hospital, you told me that God let this happen to you so
you could tell the world about Jesus. Don't you remember?"

I was speechless. I had lost all memory of those first days in the hospital. I didn't know I had said that. It seemed God was continuing the purpose He began many years earlier.

We began accepting invitations to speak, telling how God put me back together, both physically and spiritually, after that tragic day in May 1986. I was speaking at a college in Wisconsin one winter night. I was still embarrassed to show my weakness even though my tragic paralysis was at the core of our ministry. The auditorium was large with stadium seating. I normally positioned myself close to the stage so people could not see me struggle getting to the stage. That night, I was at the top of the auditorium when they called my name. I had forgotten to get in position to avoid embarrassment.

An aisle of steep steps dividing the seats led down to the stage. I nearly panicked when I realized the situation. There was no railing going down the steps! Having no other choice, I whistled to my oldest daughter, Angela, who was nine years old at the time. She quickly ran over to help me. I placed one hand on her shoulder with my other hand using my cane, and we slowly began our descent. Each step was scary. Falling would have been terrible, but it would have been much worse in front of everyone. Angela knew from years of helping me how to move one step ahead of me and stand perfectly straight so I could use her to steady myself.

We made it safely down the steps and onto the stage. My concentration was so focused on each step that I did not realize what was taking place in that auditorium as the people watched my nine-year-old daughter help me down the steps. I finally got to the stage and saw their stunned faces. I realized God was speaking to their hearts even before I said a word.

When the talk was over, I whistled for Angela again. She came running to help. Each person watched in silence. Angela's small, sturdy frame provided support to go up the steps. One by one the audience slowly stood to their feet as we stepped up higher and higher. With one hand on Angela's shoulder and one on the cane, I pushed hard one last time reaching the top. The audience erupted in applause. The message that night did not end in words. Instead, they saw a man walk up steps who was never supposed to. They saw the child of a man who was told he would never have any. They saw a man who accepted God's plan. They saw the power of God.

> *"Indeed for this purpose I have raised you up, that I may show My power in you, and that My name may be declared in all the earth."*
> — *Exodus 9:16*

About the Author

Bret Merkle is an author, speaker, and evangelist. He speaks in churches, conferences, seminars, retreats, camps, schools, prisons, and many more. Bret and his wife, Marie, founded VictoryWalk Ministries to carry out the calling that came to Bret while in the hospital in the early days after his tragic motorcycle accident:

Tell The World About Jesus

> *"The Spirit of the Lord GOD is upon me,*
> *because the LORD has anointed me to*
> *bring good news to the afflicted; He has*
> *sent me to bind up the brokenhearted, to*
> *proclaim liberty to captives, and freedom*
> *to prisoners."*   *Isaiah 61:1*

Bret has traveled throughout the US since 1998, and has gone into countries such as China, Russia, and Mexico sharing a personal message of hope as one who has been through the faith furnace touching hearts of all ages.

Bret has served on various boards as a director for ministries and businesses alike, he has been a leader of men's ministries and student ministries, and he has held various church office positions. Bret graduated from the University of South Dakota with a business degree, an MBA degree, and a law degree. When not writing or speaking, Bret works as an attorney and real estate broker in Sioux Falls, South Dakota. Bret is happily married to Marie, and together they have five children: Angela, Sarah, Ellie, Hannah, and Joshua. They live on a small ranch in eastern South Dakota.

Schedule Bret to Speak:

websites: www.tragicblessing.org or www.victorywalk.com

e-mail: contact@tragicblessing.org

Write to: PO Box 220, Harrisburg, SD, 57032

Order Tragic Blessing:

Hard and soft cover copies of Tragic Blessing can be found at www.tragicblessing.org. Order copes today and join many who use this book as a gift to a family member or friend in need of inspiration, encouragement and hope. DVD (video) and CD (audio) full length versions of Bret's talk are also available at www.tragicblessing.org.